ENGLISH LANGUAGE SKILLS

Vera Hughes

Greenwich Exchange, London

Printed and bound by Q3 Digital/Litho, Loughborough
Tel: 01509 213456
Typesetting and cover design by Albion Associates, London
Tel: 020 8852 4646

Greenwich Exchange Website: www.greenex.co.uk

ISBN 1-871551-60-9

Contents

Acknowledgements

My thanks to the OCR Examinations Board for their help and advice on their English Language examinations and the errors most frequently made in them.

My thanks, too, to my daughter, Christina, for her permission to use the spelling list and confusibles from our joint publication – *Teach Yourself The Office Handbook* by Vera and Christina Hughes, published by Hodder and Stoughton.

Finally my thanks, once again, to my partner David Weller for keying in accurately every word, full stop, comma, quotation mark etc, and for the good ideas he has allowed me to use.

Introduction

■ Is this book for you?

Did you know that in many exams and assessed schemes you lose marks if your spelling, grammar and punctuation are wrong?

Did you know that, if you are applying for a job and you make mistakes in your letter or application form, sometimes an employer will not bother to interview you?

Did you know that, when you have got a job, people get fed up with you if your English language skills are no good?

Did you know that it is not too late to do something about it?

If you want to improve your English language skills, this book is for you.

■ What will you learn from this book?

The book will remind you of the basic rules of spelling, grammar and punctuation – those things which you half learnt years ago, or have forgotten; perhaps even some things which you never learnt at all, but now need to know.

You will be able to use it as a reference book to look up odd points which you cannot quite remember, or always get wrong.

It will *not* try to teach you complicated rules about how to write English in a fancy, literary style. It will *not* use difficult words, like subjunctive or past participle; it *will* use terms like nouns, verbs and adjectives. It will *not* try to teach you the more difficult rules of English grammar; if you follow the simple notes in this book, your grammar will be acceptable.

The business and office world requires clear, accurate English: that is what this book will help you to learn, or relearn.

■ How does it work?

It works in three ways. You can work through it from beginning to end if you want to improve your English language skills all round. You will find this a useful thing to do if your skills are generally rather poor.

You can use it to work on specific points – apostrophes, for example – by looking up what you want in the Contents or Index and going straight to that part of the book.

You can also use the Practice sections in each chapter. They can be typed, word processed or hand written, and will give you practice in writing different documents in a variety of styles.

The book starts with some very basic points about writing English – the length of a sentence, when to use a new paragraph, etc. The exercises in the first few chapters are fairly easy, too.

As you work through the book, you will find that the learning goals get a little more difficult to achieve; this is partly because the English language rules themselves get more complicated, and partly because the exercises are longer and more complex. However, if you work through the chapters in order, this should not be a problem. Rules and ideas you have studied in earlier chapters are repeated in later ones, with reminders of certain basics every now and again.

None of the chapters deals with advanced or very difficult English language skills, but the exercises towards the end of the book will test your knowledge and skills quite considerably.

At the end of the book there are Appendices. Appendix 1 is a list of words which people often cannot remember how to spell. Appendix 2 is a list of words which people get confused about – their and there, for example; they are called confusibles. You will come across most of the words in Appendix 2 as you work through the book, so you will be able to practice using them, as well as being able to look them up quickly.

■ What this book is not

This is not a book which will teach you how to lay out letters, how to do summaries or answer comprehension questions. All these things are included as exercises, but there are plenty of other books to help you learn how to tackle them. This book is about grammar, spelling and punctuation: once you have decided what to write, it will help you to write it correctly.

■ About the language

English is a living language, and is changing all the time; what was accepted years ago sounds funny or wrong now. This book tries to use English which is generally acceptable to most people in English speaking countries. In doing this, there may be expressions or words which some people cannot bear to hear or read – 'different to' instead of 'different from', for example. When these expressions occur, the book will use what is still considered grammatically correct ('different from'), but may point out what is becoming generally accepted ('different to'). The author regrets any inconvenience caused while work is in progress!

1 Sentences and Paragraphs

Learning goals:
- The right length for a sentence
- Punctuating the beginnings and ends of sentences
- When to start a new paragraph
- Presentation skills
- Piece/peace
- Practice/practise

■ The right length for a sentence

'How long should a sentence be?' is rather like asking 'How long is a piece of string?' The answer is – it depends.

It depends on the idea you want to get across in a sentence, because that is the aim:

one idea = one sentence.

If you switch ideas in mid-sentence by just putting a comma and carrying on, the reader gets muddled. Read this sentence:

The meeting is scheduled to last one hour from 1100 hours, please reserve the Conference Room.

The first part of the sentence is about the time of the meeting. The second part asks the reader to book the room. The two ideas are linked, of course, but they are not the same idea. The following version is easier to read, and is therefore clearer.

The meeting is scheduled to last one hour from 1100 hours. Please reserve the Conference Room.

One good test of whether a sentence is the right length is to read it aloud. If, as you read, you find it difficult to make sense of it, that is probably because it changes ideas in the middle or because it is too long, or both. Please read the two previous examples aloud to yourself, and see which is easier to read. Business sentences are usually better if they are short and to the point.

When you are writing a sentence, ask yourself:

- Am I sticking to one idea?
- Does the sentence feel too long as I read it aloud?

You should be able to answer 'Yes' to the first question and 'No' to the second.

Exercises on sentence length

You are going to write a letter in answer to a job advertisement.

Exercise 1

1   Write the first paragraph by doing the following:
Read this sentence aloud to yourself. Try not to take a breath in the middle.

In reply to your advertisement, which I saw in the paper yesterday, I am writing to ask you to send me an Application Form because I think I would enjoy working for your company.

Is the writer sticking to one idea?
Does it feel too long as you read it aloud?
You probably answered 'No' followed by 'Yes', so the sentence needs breaking into two. Where would you break it? The best place to break it is after 'Application Form'; the writer is changing ideas at this point.

2   Write the sentences out as you think they should be written.

Exercise 2

1   Now add two sentences about the course itself:
Do the same as you did in Exercise 1:

Read the following aloud to yourself.

Ask yourself whether the writer changes ideas in mid-sentence and whether the sentence feels too long.

I am attending a full-time Office Studies course at our local college, where I am studying for the examinations mentioned in the advertisement, the results should be out by the end of August.

You probably feel the sentence is too long, but where should you break it? Decide where to make the break and then start a new paragraph and write the two sentences about the course.

2   Start another new paragraph and add two sentences of your own, expressing the following ideas:

(1) You will complete and return the Application Form as soon as you can, but you are on holiday for the next two weeks.
(2) You can go for an interview at any time once you are back home again.

3   Proofread your work by reading the whole thing aloud to yourself and by checking it against this version:

In reply to your advertisement, which I saw in the paper yesterday, I am writing to ask you to send me an Application Form. I think I would enjoy working for your company.

I am attending a full-time Office Studies course at our local college, where I am studying for the examinations mentioned in the advertisement. The results should be out by the end of August.

I will complete and return the Application Form to you as soon as possible, but I shall be away on holiday for the next two weeks. As soon as I am back, I shall be able to attend for an interview at any time.
    In those six sentences you have expressed six different ideas:

-   you are replying to the advertisement
-   you think you would enjoy working for the company
-   you are attending a course and studying for the right examinations
-   the results should be out by the end of August
-   you will be away for the next two weeks, so returning the form might be delayed
-   after that you are available for an interview.

As you work through the rest of this book, make sure:

YOUR SENTENCES EXPRESS ONE IDEA and
DO NOT SOUND TOO LONG WHEN READ ALOUD

■ Punctuating the beginnings and ends of sentences

This will be a very short section, because the rules are very simple:

ALWAYS START A SENTENCE WITH A CAPITAL LETTER

ALWAYS END A SENTENCE WITH A FULL STOP OR ITS
EQUIVALENT (QUESTION MARK OR EXCLAMATION MARK)

People sometimes forget to start with a capital letter, particularly if the first word
is I. If you are one of those people, be strict with yourself and check that *all* your
sentences start with a capital letter.

If you word processed or typed your work it was normal to leave two
spaces after a full stop - it made the typescript easier to read. You will notice
from the layout of this book that printers follow a different rule about spacing
between sentences. It is now accepted that in word processing one space is left.

■ When to start a new paragraph

Many people find it very difficult to decide when to start a new paragraph. There
is no golden rule to follow, but there are some tips which will help you.

When you start a new sentence, unless it happens to be the very first one,
ask yourself these questions:

'What have I just been writing about?'
'Is the next sentence about the same subject or topic?'

If the answer to the second question is 'Yes' – keep on with the same paragraph.
If the answer is 'No' – start a new one.

The next question is 'What do you mean by a subject or topic?'

Suppose you were writing to someone about your holiday in Corfu. What
sorts of things would you write about? Probably:

● The weather
● The food
● The night life
● The other people.

You could probably quite easily write a paragraph of three or four sentences
about each. They would be your subjects or topics. In business documents you
can do the same sort of thing.

Read the next three paragraphs from a fax sent by an Area Sales Manager and decide what each paragraph is about – its main subject, or topic.

I shall be visiting our Truro Branch on the first Tuesday of next month. I intend to arrive at about 10.00 am and stay until the close of business on the following day.

While I am in Truro I should like to go through the sales statistics for the last six months. There seems to have been an unexplained drop in sales during the first four weeks of that period. I also need to meet the people who have joined our sales force during that time, so please arrange for them to be in the office at 2.00 pm on the Wednesday.

Please book accommodation for me at the usual hotel for the Tuesday night and confirm arrangements to my Secretary.

The first paragraph is about time and dates, the second about the business to be transacted and the people to be seen, and the third about accommodation. You could almost give each paragraph a short heading:

- Date and time of visit
- Subjects of visit
- Accommodation arrangements.

Exercise on paragraphs

1   Write three paragraphs of a faxr eplying to the Area Sales Manager. As you write, think about the length of your sentences and when to start a new paragraph. This is the outline of what you should say:

Accommodation has been booked at the Crown Hotel for the Tuesday night. Usual hotel was booked up.

Sales statistics will be available first thing on Tuesday morning. You have written a Report explaining current trends.

All new sales people will be available as requested, except Brian Dunn, who will be on holiday.

2   Read aloud to yourself what you have written. Is it clear? Does it make sense? Have you included all the points? You should have written one paragraph about the hotel, one about the sales statistics and one about the sales people. Do not worry if it seems a bit short; what you are trying to do at

this point is to write fairly short, clear sentences and to make sure each paragraph deals with one subject or topic. Did each sentence start with a capital letter and end with a full stop?

As you work through this book, make sure that

WHEN YOU START A NEW TOPIC, YOU START A NEW PARAGRAPH

■ Presentation skills

Look again at the reply to the fax you have just written. What does it look like? If it is handwritten, can you read the writing? Could other people read it? Is it full of crossings out and corrections? If you keyed it in, is every word correct? Does the final result look good?

The way you present your work is *very* important. Good presentation is half the battle. Here are some rules about the presentation of business documents:

Presentation rules

1 Leave a good *margin* all the way round – 25 mm top and bottom and both sides, if possible.
2 Use *headings*, so that the reader's mind can latch on quickly to the subject or topic.
3 Leave plenty of *space* between headings, and between a heading and the text. Do not squash everything up at the top of the page.
4 Make sure your *handwriting* or *printout* is clear.
5 Be *consistent* in numbering paragraphs and pages, in the style of your headings (capital letters, emboldening etc) and in the amount of space you leave.

There are not many rules – only 5 – but if you follow all these every time you write something or print it out, your work will look really good, and people will want to read it.

Look at the exercises you have done so far. Did you follow all these rules, only some of them, or perhaps none at all?

From now on, make up your mind to present everything as well as you can. It really does make a difference.

■ Piece/peace

In this section you are going to study two sets of confusibles: piece/peace and practice/practise.

> Piece = a bit or a part
> Peace = the absence of war or noise

If you cannot remember which is which, think of the phrase 'Bits and pieces'. The word 'bit' starts 'bi' and the word 'piece' starts 'pi' when it means a 'bit'. So *bits* and *pi*eces go together. If p-i-e-c-e means a bit, p-e-a-c-e must be the other one (the absence of war or noise).

Exercise on piece/peace

Write out the following two sentences, filling in either 'piece(s)' or 'peace' where the blanks are:

A   Although _____ had been declared, there were still bits and _____ of tanks strewn around the desert.

B   I'll give you a _____ of my mind, if I don't get some _____ and quiet.

'Bits and pieces' is the key to remembering that one.

■ Practice/practise

> Practice = with a 'c' is the noun
> Practise = with an 's' is the verb (when you are actually doing it)

You can see from the definition above that you should use practice spelt with a 'c' and practise spelt with an 's' on different occasions. There is a difference between them in English, although the Americans use only the 'practise' version.

    If you cannot remember or decide which is a noun and which is a verb, here is the key to remembering this one:

Think of the words advice and advise (see Appendix 2), which you pronounce differently like this:

● I am going to give you some advice about . . .
● I am going to advise you about . . .

These two are much easier to get right because of the way in which they are pronounced.

When you come across 'practice' or 'practise', think of 'advice' or 'advise', and try to substitute either 'advice' or 'advise' for the word practi(c/s)e. For example:

- It is good (advi?) practi? to . . .

Would you use 'advice' or 'advise' there? Of course you would use 'advice' with a 'c' (even if it does not quite make sense). If you would use advice with a 'c', you must use practice with a 'c'.

- I cannot (advi?) practi? tonight because . . .

Would you use advice or advise? 'Advise' is the right answer, so you know you must use practise with an 's'.

Practice/advice
Practise/advise

Exercise on practice/practise

Write out two sentences, filling in the blanks with practice or practise. Substitute advice or advise to help you.

A He came to see me yesterday for some football _____ .
B When you _____ your drums, you'll find it's good _____ to do it in the garden shed.

You might find it difficult to remember, but now you know where to find it, you can always look it up – practice/advice
practise/advise

Now practise what you have learnt so far.

Practice

Practice 1

1 Read through the page of the Report printed below.
2 Write or key it yourself, doing the following:
   2.1 Decide on how you will present the piece – margins, headings, space, neatness.
   2.2 Divide the Report into three paragraphs.
      Give each paragraph one of the headings provided.
      Choose your own style for the headings (capital letters, emboldened etc).
   2.3 Check each sentence to make sure:
       ● it contains only one idea
       ● it does not sound too long when read aloud.
      If it is not right, correct it.

   2.4 Check that you have started each sentence with a capital letter and ended it with a full stop.
   2.5 Each time you come across peace, piece, practice or practise, check whether it is correctly spelt. If not, correct it. The words are **emboldened** so you cannot miss them.
3 Make sure you do not make mistakes in copying the text.

REPORT ON THE USE OF THE MUSIC ROOMS
The Committee considered the times at which the music rooms were used for individual **practise** and when they were used for the whole group to **practise** together. It was found that most people wanted to use the rooms at the same time, towards the end of the afternoon. This meant that individuals could not find the **peace** and concentration they needed because of the noise made by the group as a whole. The Committee found that the storage space was not being used properly and **peaces** of music were lying all over the floor. The storage lockers are adequate if correctly used, the musical instruments were damaged because they were not put away properly and were muddled up with the music stands. The Committee recommends that everyone who uses the music rooms for individual **practise** should fill in a questionnaire stating the most convenient times for using the rooms during working hours. It also recommends that members of staff from the music department should supervise more closely the storage of instruments and music stands.

Headings: **PRACTICE** TIMES
                  STORAGE FACILITIES
                  RECOMMENDATIONS

Practice 2

Write a short Report on the shop you think is the best in your area. It does not matter what it sells.

1   Think about the presentation of your Report
2   Keep your sentences short, to the point and properly punctuated
3   Use the headings given and cover all the points under each heading

Use simple business English. Do not use long words just because they look good. On the other hand do not use slang words like 'great', 'dodgy' and 'brilliant'. Advertisements use this type of word, but it is not appropriate to use them in business English.

SHOPPING AT (NAME OF SHOP)
Range of stock
What does the shop sell? Does it sell a wide range of products or only a limited range? How good is the quality of what it sells, and what are its prices like?
General atmosphere
Are the staff helpful, snooty, rude, friendly? Is it busy or peaceful? What is the lighting like? Is there any background music?

Position
Is it in the centre of things or stuck away in a side street? Is it easy to get to? Any parking facilities?

Conclusion
Your main reasons for considering it to be the best shop in your area.

Points to remember from this chapter

- A sentence is about one idea. Do not change it in the middle.
- Do not write sentences which sound too long when read aloud. Break them up.
- Start a sentence with a capital letter. End it with a full stop or its equivalent.

- A paragraph is a collection of sentences which could go under one heading.
- Use margins, space and good presentation to make your work easy to read.
- *Bits* and *pieces*
- Practice/advice
  Practise/advise

2 Full Stops and Commas

Learning goals:
- Full stops and their equivalents (question marks and exclamation marks)
- The only definite rules about commas
- You and I/you and me
- Accept/except

■ Full stops and their equivalents

In the previous chapter you were checking that you had remembered to finish every sentence with a full stop. That is the main purpose of a full stop – to end a sentence.

Some sentences need to end with a different punctuation mark – a question mark or an exclamation mark.

Question marks

When do you use a question mark? The answer seems obvious – you use a question mark when you have asked a question. 'When do you use a question mark' itself asks a question, so the sentence needs to end with a question mark, not a full stop. You must not use both, because a question mark takes the place of a full stop – in fact the full stop is part of the design of a question mark.

The problem is that some people forget to use a question mark when they should do so, and sometimes it is hard to decide whether a sentence is a question or not.

Do the following sentences need a question mark or not? The end of each sentence has deliberately been left without its punctuation mark.

A Will you be able to attend the meeting on Monday
B I know you will be able to attend the meeting on Monday
C Would you attend the meeting on Monday, please

The answer to sentence A must be 'Yes'. The reader is definitely being asked whether s(he) can attend the meeting.

The answer to sentence B must be 'No'. The reader is not being asked whether s(he) can attend; the writer is saying s(he) knows the reader will be able to attend.

The answer to sentence C is not so easy. The reader is being asked, or even ordered, to attend, but the order is put in the form of a question. So should sentence C have a question mark or not? The answer is – it does not matter! It is quite acceptable to write this sort of sentence (where a command or request is given in the form of a question) with or without a question mark. So you could say: 'If in doubt, leave it out'.

You cannot go far wrong if you use this rule about question marks:

IS THE SENTENCE A DEFINITE QUESTION
(not a wish, a hope or a command)

If the answer is 'Yes', use a question mark. If the answer is 'No', you need not use one.

Exercise on question marks

Write or key these sentences, finishing each with a full stop or a question mark, but not both! Please write this rather than doing it in your head, because it gives you good practice in copying accurately.

A How many miles are there between camping sites
B Would you like to know how many miles there are between camping sites
C You might want to know how many miles there are between camping sites
D Would you let Phil know how many miles there are between camping sites
E Count the miles between camping sites, except those in Gwent

Exclamation marks

You use an exclamation mark when you want to exclaim. When you were very young you probably read sentences like '"Goodness me!" exclaimed the baby bear.' That is an obvious use of an exclamation mark.

It is unlikely that you would want to write that sort of thing in business English, unless you are writing scripts or dialogue. Sometimes, though, you want to emphasise that what you are saying is a bit odd, a bit out of the ordinary, or even a bit rude! The exclamation mark the writer has just used shows that s(he) wrote something a little unusual – the very thought that you might write something rude in business English.

If you look back to the answer to sentence C above you will read 'The answer is – it does not matter!' This is not, perhaps, the sort of answer you would have expected – it is surprising, or unusual – so an exclamation mark was used.

Some people pepper their writing with exclamation marks, which is a pity, because *everything* then becomes surprising, or unusual. Their exclamation marks lose some weight. Save your exclamation marks for the times when you really want to show that you have written something unusual or surprising – when you want to exclaim, in fact.

Exercise on exclamation marks

Write, type or word process these sentences, using a full stop, a question mark or an exclamation mark at the end of each.

   A Would you like us to send you a brochure about camping in Scotland

   B Please complete the tear-off slip and return it to us

   C Camping in Scotland can be a wonderful holiday – even when it rains

---

Full stops not at the end of a sentence

There are two main uses of full stops other than at the end of a sentence:
- to show that a word is abbreviated
- as a decimal point

Abbreviations

You will be studying the correct use of abbreviations in Chapter 12. This section is a reminder that many people still use full stops to indicate that a word is abbreviated (for example Mr., e.g., etc.). However, in most modern offices, full stops are *not* used to show an abbreviation: the words are written without any punctuation at all. This style is part of what is called open punctuation. Full stops are still used in the text of a letter or a report, but are left out in the address, in headings and in abbreviated words like Mr, Mrs, eg, etc, NB and so on.

THERE IS NO NEED TO USE A FULL STOP TO SHOW AN ABBREVIATION

Decimal points

A full stop is used as a decimal point, as you know. However, on the continent of Europe, a comma is often used instead. Have you ever watched ice skating from Germany on the television and heard the announcer say 'Fünf komma acht' ('Five point eight')?

The reason for mentioning this here is to alert you to the fact that the more we deal with our European neighbours, the more likely it is that you will come across a comma used as a decimal point.

1,456 could be 'one thousand four hundred and fifty-six' used in the UK. If it were on the Continent, it could be 'one point four five six' (three places after the decimal point, or comma).

A word to WP users: when you want to use a decimal tab, some word processing software programs allow you to change the decimal point to a comma.

Exercise on full stops and their equivalents

This is the text of a letter about a camping holiday. Copy it out by hand or key it in, inserting stops, question marks and exclamation marks. The commas are already there. Remember to include the heading.

YOUR CAMPING HOLIDAY
Thank you for your letter enquiring about our CAMP OUT holidays We have pleasure in enclosing our brochure, as requested

I am afraid it is not possible to give you accurate details of the mileage between camp sites, because it depends on your method of transport and chosen route We have a map available which shows the positions of all our current sites (ie in England and Wales), price £500 Would you like us to send you a copy

You may be interested to know that we are also establishing sites in Scotland Camping in Scotland can be a wonderful holiday – even when it rains Would you please let us know whether you are interested in a Scottish holiday, so that we can put you on our mailing list for next year

You should have inserted at least 6 full stops, including one in the price of £5.00 but none with ie. The last sentence could finish with either a question mark or a full stop – it is a request in the form of a question. If you followed the 'If in doubt, leave it out' suggestion, you will probably have used a full stop. You needed a question mark after 'copy' and an exclamation mark after 'rains'.

■ The only definite rules about commas

Are you one of those people who bespatter your work with commas, partly because you are not sure whether you should use a comma or not?

Commas are often a matter of opinion. They are used to help the reader make sense of a piece of text. When you are reading aloud, commas show where it is sensible and natural to take a breath.

There are two main instances where commas should definitely be used.

- When you are writing a list
- Round a sub-clause

Commas in lists

You probably remember that you should use commas in lists of things, except for the last two items on the list, which are joined by 'and'. For example:

'You will need an anorak, waterproof trousers, thick socks and good walking shoes.'

shows the correct use of commas in a list. Here is another sentence using commas in a list:

'The slippers she wore were soft, warm, furry and very cosy.'

This time the list is a list of adjectives (soft, warm, furry and cosy), but it still needs comas between the words except the last two in the list. (An adjective is a word which describes a noun. A noun is a naming word, so 'soft' is an adjective, 'slipper' is a noun.)

Here is another example:

'The flat will be shared by Paul, Sandra, you and me.'

USE COMMAS BETWEEN ITEMS IN A LIST
EXCEPT BETWEEN THE LAST TWO ITEMS
WHICH SHOULD BE JOINED BY 'AND'

Exercise on commas in lists

Check back on the examples, if you need to, and say where the commas should come in the following sentences:

A At this time of year the flowers in the bouquet will be roses carnations pinks and lilies.
B Scientists have found a small grey interesting blob on the slide.
C Trains for Norfolk will leave at 1000 hrs 1130 hrs 1300 hrs and 1615 hrs.

In sentence A you needed commas after 'roses' and 'carnations'.
In sentence B they are needed after 'small' and 'grey' (*not* after interesting).
In sentence C you should have put them after '1000 hrs' and '1130 hrs'.

Commas before 'and'

You probably learnt, quite rightly, that in a list you do not need a comma before the word 'and'. In the sentences you have just written, there is no comma after 'pinks' or after '1300 hrs'.

This is often one of those half-remembered rules where your brain tells you 'no comma before 'and'', so whenever you see a comma before 'and' you think it is wrong. Sometimes it *is* wrong as we saw in the simple lists; but sometimes it is right to put a comma before 'and'.

It is right to put a comma when it helps the reader to make sense of what is written. For example:

The dress was black, and white buttons made it look smart.

If you leave out the comma before the 'and', it could sound as though the dress itself was black and white.

Commas round a sub-clause

Sentences are often short, straightforward and simple, but sometimes they need to be longer and more complicated to say exactly what the writer wants to express.

'The airport lounge was crowded and unbearably hot.' is a simple sentence. If we want to add the reasons for the airport being crowded we could say:

'The airport lounge, because of the flight delays, was crowded and unbearably hot.'

The extra phrase 'because of the flight delays' is called a sub-clause. It is part of a sentence which, if left out altogether, would not alter the meaning of the sentence.

Here are some more complicated sentences. Each contains a sub-clause. See if you can pick out the sub-clause in each sentence:

A The plane when it did arrive had to be cleaned and re-fuelled.
B The passengers who were very fed up by this time still had a long wait.
C It was a great relief when the plane was ready to get on board and find their seats.
D The airline was of course most apologetic.

The sub-clauses are:

A 'when it did arrive'
B 'who were very fed up by this time'
C 'when the plane was ready'

D 'of course' is usually thought of as a sub-clause and therefore needs a pair of commas. Some people leave out the commas round 'of course' or 'however', which is acceptable. Both these phrases should have either two commas, or none.

It would probably have been easier to pick out those sub-clauses if they had commas round them like this:

A The plane, when it did arrive, had to be cleaned and re-fuelled.
B The passengers, who were very fed up by this time, still had a long wait.
C It was a great relief, when the plane was ready, to get on board and find their seats.
D The airline was, of course, most apologetic.

Those commas also make the sentences easier to read and clearer in meaning – particularly sentence C. So, to make life easier for the reader:

SUB-CLAUSES MUST HAVE A *PAIR* OF COMMAS ROUND THEM

They need a comma at the beginning of the sub-clause and a comma at the end.

TO IDENTIFY A SUB-CLAUSE, TRY READING THE SENTENCE WITHOUT THE PHRASE YOU THINK MIGHT BE A SUB-CLAUSE

IF THE SENTENCE STILL MAKES SENSE, THAT PHRASE IS A SUB-CLAUSE

Exercise on commas round a sub-clause

Write or key this fax, putting the commas round the sub-clauses. All the other punctuation is right, so you do not need to worry about it.

FLIGHT DELAYS
We have had several complaints from our clients which have been forwarded to me about flight delays. There is little we can do about this because as you will be aware we are in the hands of the Air Traffic Controllers.

Please deal with any further complaints whether they are addressed to me or not at local level. I regret I cannot reply to all our clients personally much as I would like to because of pressure of work.

Check what you have written against this correct copy: the sub-clauses and their pairs of commas are in brackets.

FLIGHT DELAYS

We have had several complaints from our clients (, which have been forwarded to me,) about flight delays. There is little we can do about this because (, as you will be aware,) we are in the hands of the Air Traffic Controllers.

Please deal with any further complaints (, whether they are addressed to me or not,) at local level. I regret I cannot reply to all our clients personally (, much as I would like to,) because of pressure of work.

If you read the fax without the sub-clauses, it makes perfectly good sense, but seems a little curt. People often put in sub-clauses to soften what they have to say.

A comma after an introductory phrase

Commas are there to help the reader. Another instance when a comma can be very helpful is after an introductory phrase like

- When he had drilled the hole, he . . .
- Having heard what you have to say, I think . . .

Such a phrase often begins with words like 'when', 'if', 'after', 'having', 'before', 'following' and 'once'.

Exercise on a comma after an introductory phrase

Write or key these sentences, putting in the commas after the introductory phrases.

A   Once you have passed through the turnstile you may not re-enter the ground.
B   When you have finished reading it please pass it on to the next person.
C   Having covered up her ears she could not hear a thing.

You should have put a comma after 'turnstile', 'reading it' and 'ears'.

It is not essential to use a comma after an introductory phrase, but it is very helpful to the reader.

Where not to use commas

Do not use commas:

- to join two sentences together. Use a full stop instead (see Chapter 1) or perhaps a semi-colon (see Chapter 10).
- in the address on a letter or envelope, if you are using open punctuation.

Mrs A Brown
104 Foster Street
BRISTOL
BS8 2HL

need not have any commas (or full stops). You do not need them after 'Dear Mrs Brown' or 'Yours sincerely' either.

Where commas must be used

When *must* you use commas? There are two instances when they must be used. Complete this sentence:

Commas must be used

a)   and

b)

If you remember those two rules, you will find your use of commas acceptable. Do not use a comma when you should use a full stop.

■ You and I/you and me

How often do you say 'Between you and I ...'? Did you know that this is *wrong*? It should be 'Between you and me ...'. Why?

This is probably a half-remembered rule which told you:

It is not good style or good English to say 'Robert and me went to the match.'. You must say 'Robert and I went to the match.'.

If that is what you have remembered, that is quite right.

The problem is that many people then transfer that rule and use it when it *should* be 'Robert and me'. For example, it is *wrong* to say 'Gary came to see Robert and I.'. The way to test this is to leave out the other person (Robert) and see whether the sentence sounds right. Would you say 'Gary came to see I.'?

Unless you live in somewhere like Somerset or Devon, where it might be part of your dialect, probably not. So you should not say 'Gary came to see (Robert and) I.'.

If you have always said and written things like 'Give that to Tracey and I.' (which is *wrong*), it will probably sound rather funny to say 'Give that to Tracey and me.', but that is the right way of saying or writing it.

For those of you who want to know the grammatical reason for this: in the sentence 'Robert and I went to the match.', Robert and I are the subject of the sentence. In the sentence 'Gary came to see Robert and me.', Robert and me are the object.

To go back to 'Between you and me', which is right, think of saying 'Between you, me and the gatepost', and you will probably get it right.

Exercise on you and I/you and me

Write, type or word process these sentences, inserting 'me' or 'I', as appropriate:

A   Please leave the key with the lady next door. Mrs Peters and _____ will pick it up.

B   Between you and _____ , I do not think the property is worth all that money.

C   Do not forget to post the Contract to Mr Wheeler or _____ by the end of the week.

D   My husband and _____ are delighted to accept your kind invitation. Please let him or _____ know the best time to arrive.

■ Accept/except

Accept = to receive or agree
Except = with the exception of

This is one of the confusibles dealt with in Appendix 2 – some people do get them confused!

The easiest way to remember which is which is to ask yourself:

'Could I use the phrase 'with the exception of' instead?'

If you could, the word you want must be 'except'. If not, it must be 'accept'. For example, in the sentence 'Everyone accept/except Jill left early,' you could easily say 'Everyone, with the exception of Jill, left early.' So it must be 'except(ion)' and not 'accept'.

Exercise on accept/except

Which would you use in the following sentence?
'The whole office wants to accept/except the invitation, accept/except John, who has better things to do.'

Practice

This chapter has been mainly about full stops and commas. Copy the following letter, and as you do so:

- Fill each punctuation blank (marked*) with a full stop, question mark, exclamation mark or comma.
- Where you see accept/except, choose the right one.
- Where you see _____ insert 'I' or 'me'.

NB 1 *Do not* put commas or full stops in the address, in Dear Mr and Mrs Cooper, after Yours sincerely or in the heading.
2 Block everything to the left, as it is printed here. This is the normal layout for letters in a modern office.
3 Remember to leave a good margin each side.

Mr and Mrs D Cooper
8 Farthing Avenue
DURHAM
DH2 4JN

Dear Mr and Mrs Cooper

21 Horseferry Road

We have pleasure in confirming that we are nearly ready to exchange
Contracts for the purchase of the above property* We have all the papers
we need accept/except those we sent to you last week*

Please arrange to let us have* as soon as possible* your copy of the
Contract* the Schedule of Fixtures and Fittings* and your cheque for the
balance of the deposit* Would you please make sure that all the papers
are signed*

The Vendors are happy to accept/except your suggested completion date*
Would you like me to write to their Solicitors confirming that date* New
year's Eve is an unusual day to move house* but you will be able to drink
to your new home before the New Year begins*

I am anxious that there should be no further delay in this matter* so
please address your letter to both Mr A Andrews and _____* If you
address it as I have suggested Mr Andrews and _____ are both
likely to see it and deal with it promptly*

Yours sincerely

Naomi Morris (Mrs)
Partner

Points to remember from this chapter

- Use a question mark when you have asked a definite question.
- Use an exclamation mark when you have written something surprising or unusual.
- You do not need to use full stops in abbreviations; you do not need full stops or commas in addresses on letters etc.
- Full stops are used as decimal points; on the Continent they sometimes use a comma instead.
- Use commas in lists, except for the last two items joined by 'and'.
- It is not always wrong to use a comma before 'and'.
- Use a pair of commas round a sub-clause.
- 'Between you and I' is *always* wrong.
- Leave out the other person to test whether it should be 'I' or 'me'.
- If you can substitute 'with the exception of' it must be 'except' not 'accept'.

3 Complete Sentences

Learning goals:
- Writing a complete sentence
- A subject
- A verb
- Of/off
- Of/have

■ Writing a complete sentence

A complete sentence must always have a SUBJECT and a VERB. This is a strict rule: if you follow it, you cannot be wrong. What is a subject and what is a verb?

A subject

The word 'subject' here is a technical term. It does not mean 'topic', as we used it earlier. The subject of a sentence is the person or thing which is actually doing or being what the sentence is describing. Here are some examples of complete sentences. In each case the subject is in brackets:

A (We) ran.
B (A Manager) can be male or female.
C When he had finished one task, (the Trainee) started the next.
D In spite of the intense heat, (the firefighters) played on the burning instruments for hours.

To identify the subject of a sentence, ask yourself:

WHO OR WHAT IS ACTUALLY DOING OR BEING SOMETHING?

Exercise on identifying the subject

Which is the subject of each of these sentences?

A The paper got jammed in the photocopier again.
B For the fourth time that week, the Office Manager called the engineer.
C The engineer sorted it out yet again.
D Eventually we were all able to get our photocopying done.

The subjects you picked out should have been 'the paper', 'the Office Manager', 'the engineer' and 'we'.

Many sentences are much more complicated than those, but the question still holds good. In fact the sentence you have just read has two subjects – 'many sentences' and 'the question', there are two mini sentences joined by 'but'. Have you noticed anything about all the subjects we have identified? The subjects have been:

We; Manager; the Trainee; the firefighter; the paper; the Office Manager; the engineer; we; many sentences; the question.

They are all nouns (a word which names something, like a Manager, the Trainee) or pronouns (we). A *subject is usually* a *noun* or pronoun. We say 'usually' because it can be a phrase; in a sentence like 'mending the photocopier is a boring job', 'mending the photocopier' is the subject of that sentence.

THE SUBJECT OF A SENTENCE IS THE PERSON OR THING WHICH ACTUALLY DOES OR IS SOMETHING

A COMPLETE SENTENCE MUST HAVE A SUBJECT AND A VERB

A verb

A verb is a doing or being word. This is one of the technical terms you probably remember. Below you will find listed all the sentences you have just been working on. In the first four the verb has been written in italics. In the other six see if you can identify the verb: write the sentences out with the subject in brackets and underline the verb.

The subjects are in brackets; it is easier to pick out the main verb in a sentence if you identify the subject first. In each case ask yourself:

'WHAT DID THE SUBJECT ACTUALLY SAY, DO OR BE?'

A   (We) *ran.*

B   (A Manager) *can be* male or female.

C   When he had finished one task, (the Trainee) *started* the next.

D   In spite of the intense heat, (the firefighters) *played* on the burning instruments for hours.

E   (The paper) got jammed in the photocopier again.

F   For the fourth time that week, (the Office Manager) called the engineer.

G   (The engineer) sorted it out yet again.

H   Eventually (we) were all able to get our photocopying done.

I   (Many sentences) are much more complicated than those, but (the question) still holds good.

J   (Mending the photocopier) is a boring job.

The words you should have underlined are:

got jammed; called; sorted out; were able; are; holds good; is.

You will see that the verbs are not all one word, but do not worry about that. The important thing is to find the verb, or at least part of it, to prove that the sentence is complete.

A SENTENCE MUST HAVE A SUBJECT AND A VERB

Exercise on complete sentences

1   The following are all complete sentences. Write or key them, putting the subject in brackets and underlining the main verb.

A   Fire drills are an important part of fire safety.

B   When the fire bell goes, everyone should stop working and go out quickly.

C   Fortunately, the music shop had carried out its fire drills.

D   So when a fire did occur, staff and customers got out safely.

E   In spite of the intense heat, the firefighters played on the burning instruments for hours.

2   Some of these are complete sentences, and some are not. Pick out those which are *not* complete sentences.

   A   In reply to your letter of 8 January.
   B   We acknowledge receipt of your application form.
   C   Regular income, security, good prospects.
   D   Introducing the latest personal computer.
   E   Or fully automatic timing devices.
   F   The latest money supply figures, showing a record rise in bank and building society lending, were less encouraging.

Only B and F are complete sentences. A, D and E have neither subject nor verb; C has three subjects but no verb. C, D and E are all from adverts, which are notoriously bad at writing complete sentences. We shall be looking at special forms of writing in Chapter 13. In the meantime, try not to copy the ads!

If you are trying to decide whether what you have written is a complete sentence or not, try reading it aloud. For example, 'In reply to your letter of 8 January.' read aloud leaves you in midair. Read C, D and E aloud, and you will find the same thing happens.

The answers to question 1 are (you should have underlined the word(s) in italics):

A   (fire drills) *are*
B   (everyone) *should stop working* and *go out* (If you underlined only *should*, you identified part of the verbs, which is enough to prove the sentence is complete.)
C   (the music shop) *had carried out*
D   (staff and customers) *got out* (Yes, a subject can be plural)
E   (the firefighters) *played*

A COMPLETE SENTENCE MUST HAVE A SUBJECT AND A VERB.

■ Of/off

of   = belonging to
off   = away from

Many people get muddled over the use of 'of' and 'off', so this section will try to make it clear.

The easiest way is to know for sure when you should use 'off'. If you are sure about that, you know you must use 'of' every other time you come across it.

When to use 'off'

You use 'off' whenever you want to say that something is coming or going or being taken *away* from something. These are the sorts of expressions which use 'off':

- The child fell off the wall.
- The aircraft takes off.
- Come off it!
- The cheese smelt a bit off.
- The car is a write-off.

You can probably think of an expression which includes the word 'off' and which means 'Go away!', but this is not the place to write it!
    If you read all those expressions aloud, the 'off' *always* sounds as if it has two f's - and so it has. ('Of' sounds as though it is spelt 'ov'.)

IF THE EXPRESSION IS ABOUT BEING *AWAY* FROM
SOMETHING, OR IF YOU SAY IT WITH TWO Fs, USE 'OFF'

Exercise on of/off

Type or key this paragraph, inserting 'of' or 'off' wherever you see 'o- - -':

Our visitors will be leaving the building at 1630 hours. Please arrange for someone to see them o- - - at the airport. The plane is due to take o- - - at 2000 hours, so they will need to leave promptly to take account o- - - possible delays on the motorway. They will need plenty o- - - time to check in at the airport. I regret we cannot pay overtime to the person escorting them to the airport, but you may grant time o- - - in lieu.

■ Of/have

People often make the mistake of writing 'of' when it should be 'have'. This is sometimes because we speak in a rather lazy way, and say a word like 'uv'. Read these expressions aloud:

- We should've gone.
- Would you like to 'uv' bought that?
- Don't tell me you could 'uv' done it.

When you are chatting to one another, it does not matter if you use a word which sounds like 'uv'. If you are trying to speak more formally (in a meeting, for example) or to write, it is *wrong* to say or write 'should of', 'could of', 'like to of'. Some of you might find it difficult to *say* 'might *have*' or 'could *have*', because of having to pronounce the 'h', but you should not find it difficult to *write* 'will have' or 'cannot have'.

For those of you who want to know why 'should of etc is wrong, it is because you are using the wrong part of speech. 'Have' is part of the past tense of the verb you are using:

'I walk' is present tense
'*I have* walked' is past tense
'I can' is present
'I could *have*' is past.

The same applies to 'might have', 'should have', 'to have bought' etc.

The word 'of' shows possession, and is nothing to do with the past tense at all. 'The back of the bike', 'the amount of money' and 'top of the pile' are all expressions which show possession - nothing to do with the past tense of a verb.

'HAVE' IS PART OF A VERB; 'OF' SHOWS POSSESSION

Exercise on of/have

Read this extract from a letter aloud to yourself. Each time you come across the word 'of' or 'have', stop and ask yourself whether it is right or wrong.

Thank you for your letter *of* 29 May, and for the enclosures which we found full *of* interest.

34

Perhaps when you *have* considered the plans more fully, you will be able to take a firm decision on the siting *of* the new branch. We appreciate that you could not *of* done this sooner, because *of* the time factor. We might *have* been able to get the plans to you earlier if we had received the proposals ourselves.

Practice

Type or key the following Notice; you will find it contains several mistakes:

- some sentences are incomplete
- sometimes 'of' is used when it should be 'off'
- sometimes 'off' is used when it should be 'of'
- sometimes 'of' is used when it should be 'have'.

When you find the incomplete sentences, alter them to make them complete. Every time you come to 'of', 'off' or 'have', check whether it is right and correct it if it is wrong.

NOTICE

KEEP OF THE GRASS

Members of the public are warned not to walk, eat or sleep on the grass. Because of its position. This patch off grass is our best piece of lawn right in front of the house. If you could of seen the state it was in last summer. You would not have been surprised to read this Notice now. It had high-heel marks all over it, people had left a lot of their picnic wrappings on it and some people had even snuggled down and dropped of to sleep in the middle of it. So, please, we say again –

KEEP OF THE GRASS

Points to remember from this chapter

- A sentence must have a *subject* and a *verb*. If it does not have both it is not a sentence.
- 'Off' is concerned with being *away*, and is pronounced as if it had two fs, which it has.
- 'Of' is a word which shows possession.
- Expressions like 'should of come', 'might of liked' are *wrong*: it should be 'should *have* come', 'might *have* liked'.

4 Three Basic Spelling Rules

Learning goals:
- i before e
- Plurals of nouns ending in 'y'
- Doubled consonants
- Two/to/too
- Affect/effect

■ Spelling rules

It is odd that many people seem quite proud of the fact that they cannot spell properly. At work it is important to get the spelling right, because the written work you send out is part of the image of your company or organisation.

If you are a bad speller, working through one chapter of this book is not going to cure your disability overnight, but there are several things you can do to help yourself. In Appendix 1 there is a list of words which people often get wrong; you can use this list to check those spellings, or you can use the spellchecker on your word processor. Anything you can do to improve your spelling is well worth the effort – and it will need quite a lot of effort if you think you have a mental block about spelling.

English is not the easiest language in the world to spell correctly, but there are some basic rules which, if you know them thoroughly, will help with some of the spelling difficulties. In this chapter you will be studying three basic rules.

I before e

Do you remember the rule 'I before E except after C'? Do you also remember that the rule should go on to say '. . . but only when it rhymes with key'? The whole rule is:

I BEFORE E EXCEPT AFTER C, BUT ONLY WHEN IT RHYMES WITH KEY

This means that we do not have to bother about words like 'beige', 'height' or 'leisure'. What we do have to think about is any word which contains the two vowels 'ie' or 'ei' together when they sound like ee. The i comes before the e (as in believe) except after a c, when they are written the other way round (as in received).

This is a good rule because it is very nearly foolproof: there are only four exceptions:

seize; weir; weird; protein

and some proper names like Leith (a port in Scotland) and Reid.

If you learn this rule and get it right, it should solve several of your spelling problems.

Exercise on i before e

Keep the rule firmly in mind and write or key the following paragraph. Where you see ( ) in a word, insert ie or ei. If you are using a word processor, do not use the spellchecker.

Thank you for your br( )f letter, which we only rec( )ved yesterday. I bel( )ve you posted it the week before last, but as you can see, it has only just arrived.

I was rel( )ved to hear that Malcolm has been cleared of all blame. Nobody now can think of him as a common th( )f, although he did dec( )ve one or two people. He should not have pretended the re( )pt was his.

Please give him our best wishes, and tell him we hope he ach( )ves good results in his exams.

Check carefully that you have written brief, received, believe, relieved, thief, deceive, receipt and achieve. It is very easy to miss mistakes.

Plurals of nouns ending in 'y'

Another very good rule is the one about the plurals of nouns ending in y. This rule is pretty well foolproof, too. It is:

TO MAKE A PLURAL OF NOUNS ENDING IN Y,
CHANGE THE Y INTO I AND ADD ES
WHEN THE LETTER BEFORE THE Y IS A CONSONANT

This rule really does work, but the last line written above is very important. A good example of this is:

STORY – plural STORIES
The last letter before the Y is a consonant,
so change the Y to an I and add ES.
STOREY (part of a building) – plural STOREYS
The last letter before the Y is a vowel,
so to make the plural, just add an S.

Another example is TROLLY and TROLLEY. It depends on how you spell the word when it is singular, and either version is acceptable.

Singular TROLLY = plural TROLLIES
Singular TROLLEY = plural TROLLEYS
(TROLLYS is definitely wrong)

Incidentally, talking about consonants and vowels, you know that what is not a vowel (a, e, i, o, or u) must be a consonant. The word is CONSONANT, not CONS*T*ONANT as some people say.

Exercise on the plural of y words

In this extract from the Minutes of a Meeting, all the nouns ending in y are emboldened. They are written in the singular, but you must put them in the plural as you write or key the following:

OPENING PROGRAMME

It was agreed to ask two **personality** to open the **factory** at the end of March. The building in Carlisle has four **storey**, but the one in Stockton-on-Tees has only two. The military band is to be asked to play tunes from 'All Our

Yesterday' at the start of the day, but to progress to more modern, upbeat music as the day draws towards the climax of the official opening.

The **lady** are to be presented with **spray** of flowers. Fruit juices and **sherry** will be served to guests as they enter the reception area.

Check that what you have written is personalities, factories, storeys, Yesterdays, ladies, sprays and sherries. If you stick firmly to the rule, you will have found that it does work. (NB will *have* found, not *of* found!)

Doubled consonants

Do you often have to stop and wonder whether it is two m's or one, or two t's or s's? There are various rules which can help you decide this, but unfortunately they are not all foolproof - there are exceptions. Most of the spellings stick to the rules, so it is helpful to learn them anyway.

There are three main rules about doubled consonants, which occur in different types of word:

1   Listen to the sound of the consonant
2   Listen to the sound of the vowel before the consonant
3   Double the consonant and add the ending.

We will take each one separately.

1   *Listen to the sound of the consonant*
This is mostly about f's and s's, because they are pronounced differently depending on whether there is one or two of them. We have already seen this with 'of' and 'off'.

A double *f* flanked by two vowels must be pronounced like an f, as in office, offer, buffer, toffee, or differ. So why do we not write 'iff' or 'proffess'? We said there were exceptions! The rule holds good for 'difficult' and 'difference'.

In the same way double s is pronounced s, while the single s is usually pronounced z (as in as or is!). Think of words like mess, toss, dress and caress. Following this rule makes it easier to spell words like assess, assessment or professor. Next time you wonder 'how many s's in assessment?', think of this pronunciation rule, and you will probably get it right.

ff sounds like f	ss sounds like s
f sounds like v	s sounds like z

How many f's or s's would you put in the **emboldened** words?

A   The rest of the answer was all **wa?le**.
B   **Pa?** me the list of names and **addre?es**, please.
C   **Ru?les** on skirts and shirts are in this year.
D   Sexual **hara?ment** can make life miserable at work.
E   Talk about **embarra?ing**!
F   Did you **tran?fer** the moneys **succe?fully?**
G   What **po?e?ed** you to **mi?** the **occa?ion?**

There is only one word in these sentences which does not follow the rule – it only half follows it – and that is 'possessed'. You might think it should be spelt posessed, but that would be wrong. As we said, there are exceptions!

2   *Listen to the sound of the vowel before the consonant*
This rule applies for many consonants. The easiest thing to do is to learn a good example and apply the rule when you get stuck over other consonants.

A good example is COMA and COMMA. With only one m the o is what is called 'long', pronounced ō as in rope. With two m's the vowel before the m, the o, is a 'short' o, and pronounced o as in lot. Doubling the consonant has the effect of shortening the vowel. Here are some more examples:

cope and copper;
ruse and Russian;
life and Liffey (the river in Dublin);
raged and ragged.

You probably remember that putting an 'e' on the end of a word alters the pronunciation of the preceding vowel; it makes a short vowel long.

mad becomes made   rag becomes rage
pet becomes Peter   met becomes mete
kit becomes kite   trip becomes tripe
Tom becomes tome   lob becomes lobe
cur becomes cure   bus becomes abuse

The doubled consonant has the opposite effect; it makes a long vowel short. Here are some more examples:

rated and ratted
moped and mopped (moped here means sulked, not a small motorbike)
write and written
siting and sitting

41

With this in mind, where there is a ?, say whether there should be a single or double consonant, as you did in the previous sentences A-G.

H   Please book the hotel **acco(m?)odation**.
I   It was a **ha(p?)y** time.
J   The **Co(m?)i(t?)ee** approved the Minutes.
K.   Would you **reco(m?)end** this company?

In each case the consonant should be doubled. If you had only a single c, m, p or t, it would alter the pronunciation of the vowel before it, and would sound very odd indeed.

3   *Double the consonant and add the ending*
Unfortunately this rule is not foolproof either, but it is often helpful.

IF YOU WANT TO ADD 'ED' OR 'ING' TO A WORD
WHICH ENDS IN ONE VOWEL, CONSONANT –
DOUBLE THE CONSONANT AND ADD THE ENDING

Here are some examples:

commit → committed → committing;
occur → occurred → occurring;
refer → referred → referring.

There are quite a few words which are exceptions to this rule, some of these are:

benefited, benefiting	remembered, remembering
budgeted, budgeting	sponsored, sponsoring
opened, opening	targeted, targeting

The following words all obey the rule 'double the consonant and add the ending', so how would you spell the following with 'ed' or 'ing' on the end? (Some will not take 'ed' as an ending.)

omit; transmit; defer; jam; plan; star; stir; cram; begin;
forget; regret; spur; fulfil; equip.

There are more words which follow this rule than words which do not, so it is worth remembering. If in doubt, look the word up in the dictionary. A good dictionary will tell you if the spelling for different endings is unusual.

Exercise on doubling the consonant

This is a page from a procedure manual, in which you will find emboldened words which may or may not need doubled consonants. Some of them are right and some are wrong. Write or key the page, making sure the **emboldened** words are right. The other words are right, so you can concentrate on the doubled consonants.

HOW TO OPERATE YOUR PHOTOCOPIER

1   Lift the lid over the **glass** plate and **possition** the work to be copied face down on the plate.
2   Before **shuting** the lid, make sure the paper is in the **correct** position. Take note **off** the **buffer** zone at the top and side of the page; check that no typing will be **omited** from the copy.
3   Tell the photocopier how many copies you require. **Forgeting** to do this at the **beginning** of the operation can waste a lot **of** time.
4   **Pres** the green key.
5   If the paper gets **jamed** in the machine, **follow** the instructions to release it.
6   Check that you have the right number **of** copies and that they are all of good quality.
7   It has often **occured** that the master copy is left in the machine. REMEMBER TO REMOVE YOUR MASTER COPY.

This is the right way to spell the emboldened words; they are in alphabetical order:

beginning; buffer; correct; follow; forgetting; glass; jammed; occurred; of; omitted; position; press; shutting.

■ Two/to/too

Two = 2
To   = part of a verb or to(wards)
Too = also or too much of (over the top)

The most common mistake people make is to write 'to' when it should be 'too'. An easy way to remember this is that when *too* means als*o* it needs the extra o. When it means OTT (*over the top*) it also needs the extra o.

To remember that 2 = two, think of twice or twins (or twain, if you are Scottish). *Twice* begins with *tw*, and so does two when it means 2.

On every other occasion, it must be plain t - o.

'To' is part of a verb (to go, to do, to have etc) – it is actually called the infinitive. A verb is a doing word, as we know, so if you think of 'to do', it might help you *to* remember that one.

Exercise on two/to/too

Here is a silly poem. Every time you see t - -, decide whether it should be two, to or too.

T – – worms met on a spiral staircase
And one t – – the other one said:
'I can't think what I'm going t – – do.
'Do you have the trouble that I have, t – –?
'Every time I want t – – go up
'I go back down instead.'

There is one 'two' and one 'too'. All the others are 'to'.

■ Affect/effect

Affect = the verb (*a*ctually doing it)
Effect = normally the noun

It is not always easy to decide whether the word you are using is a noun or a verb. In this case you can ask yourself whether the person or thing concerned is *a*ctually doing it; if the answer is 'Yes', it must be the verb.

Exercise on affect/effect

In this paragraph from a fax, decide each time you see [   ] whether the word to be inserted should be affect or effect. Ask yourself whether the person or thing is *a*ctually doing it.

I am returning this tape to be re-recorded because I am not happy about the sound [   ]. The sound of the closing door is much to*o* heavy; it has the [   ] of making this scene sound as if it is in a mansion rather than an ordinary home.

We shall not expect the re-recording to [   ] the cost of the tape. We did not specify the scene setting in the first place.

You should have two 'effects' followed by an 'affect'. Incidentally did you know that in the recording world sound effects are written FX?

Note: 'Effect' with an e can sometimes be a verb; when it is, it means making something happen (to effect a reconciliation, effect an entry, for example).

Finally, apply the rules to this newspaper advertisement, and decide whether Little Cherub got it right:

LITTLE CHERUB PHOTOGRAPHERS
Little Cherub Photographers
would like to apologise for any
inconvenience caused to the
customers who attended our

Photo Competition at the Little
Cherub clothes shops when the
competition had to be cancelled.
We will be offering a FREE home
sitting for those customers
effected.

Practice

Practice 1

This is another page from the manual about how to get the best out of your
photocopier. Key or write the page correcting any errors.
This time they are not marked, so you will have to find them.
    The errors are likely to be:

- ie or ei written incorrectly
- the plurals of nouns ending in y incorrectly spelt
- double consonants when they should be singular and vice versa
- the wrong form of two, to or too
- affect or effect incorrectly used.

There are ten errors to find and correct as you copy the paper.

HOW TOO OPERATE YOUR PHOTOCOPIER

Double-sided copying
Double-sided copying is done when you want the work copied onto both
sides of the paper. The procedure applies to any size of paper. It is for use
when the opperation cannot be done automatically.

1   Make the required number of copys on one side of the paper as normal.
2   Transfer the copies from the recieving tray to the feeder tray by picking
    them up, turning them over and puting them in the feeder tray *the same
    way round.*
    Transfering them in this way ensures that the back of the page will not
    come out upside down.

3 Lift the lid over the glass plate. Turn the master copy over but not round, *or*, place the second master copy face down on the glass plate *the same way round* as the previous master.
4 Close the lid and make *one* copy to check that all is well.
5 Tell the photocopier the number of copies you need. Press the green key.
6 If the paper gets jamed, you will have lost one or two sheets of paper. This will effect the number of completed copies. You will have to few copies off side one as well as side two, and will have to do some more to compensate.
7 Check that you have the right number of double-sided copies.

Practice 2

1 You are the Office Manager writing a Memorandum to the Word Processing Supervisor. Give the Memo today's date and the reference OS/COP.
   If you have no Memorandum paper, use ordinary A4 paper and make your headings like this:

MEMORANDUM

To:	Reference:
From:	Date:

A Memorandum is not usually signed.

2 The Memo is about PHOTOCOPYING PROCEDURES, so on the next line write this in as the heading to your Memo.

These are the points you want to make in the Memo:

● you have noticed that the quality of the photocopying is not as good as it should be
● you are enclosing two pages of instructions which you would like the WP Supervisor to pin up near the machine
● you will be keeping a close watch on the quality in the future

3 Make sure you use the following expressions in your Memorandum. The words in square brackets may or may not be right; check them and write them correctly.

   'It has been brought [to] my [atention]'
   'I have [recieved] several complaints'
   'The [copies] are [to] faint'

'Please make sure they are [pined] up near the machine'
'Poor-quality [copies] [effect] the Company image'
'I [believe] the machine has been serviced recently'
'There should be fewer [inaccuracys]'

4   Write short sentences and make sure the Memo is divided into relevant
    paragraphs. Check your punctuation. Make sure the layout looks good. Use
    straightforward English, but not slang.

Points to remember from this chapter

- i before e except after c but only when it rhymes with key
- For the plural of nouns ending in y
  when the letter before the y is a consonant
  CHANGE THE Y INTO I AND ADD ES
- Listen to the sound of f's and s's
- ff = f   ss = s
- f = v   s = z
- Listen to the sound of the vowel before the consonant
  COMA AND COMMA
  To shorten the vowel, double the consonant
- To add 'ed' or 'ing' to a word which ends
  one vowel, consonant
  DOUBLE THE CONSONANT AND ADD THE ENDING
- T*W*O = 2 (T*W*INS)
  TO   =   part of a verb (TO DO) or
           TO(wards)
  TOO =   als*o* or to*o* much (*O*TT)
- AFFECT – is it *a*ctually doing it? (the verb)
  EFFECT – the noun (sound FX)

5 Singulars and Plurals

Learning goals:
- Making the verb agree with the subject
- The verb 'to be'
- Collective nouns
- Personnel/personal
- Lend/borrow

■ Making the verb agree with the subject

In Chapter 3 to make sure a sentence was complete you were identifying the subject of the sentence and the verb. Another reason for being able to identify which is the subject and which is the verb is that the verb must agree with its subject.

A SINGULAR SUBJECT needs a SINGULAR VERB

A PLURAL SUBJECT needs a PLURAL VERB

This is a very firm rule; the problem is that it is not always easy to decide whether the subject is singular or plural. We will start with some straightforward examples.

One woman waits for the train.
Two women wait for the train.

'One woman' must be singular, so the verb is singular, and you say or write 'waits'. You do this without thinking, and probably never get it wrong.
In the same way 'Two women' must be plural, and so the verb is plural – 'wait'.
There are times when it is much more difficult to decide whether the subject is singular or plural. These times are likely to be:

- when the subject is two nouns joined by 'and'
- when the subject is two nouns joined by 'or'
- when the subject is two nouns joined by and/or
- when the subject sounds plural but is, in fact, singular.

We will take each one separately.

When the subject is two nouns joined by 'and'

Sometimes it is quite easy to get the verb right. For example, in the sentence

One woman and one man wait for the train.

'One woman and one man' must be plural (more than one), so the verb, too, must be plural – they 'wait'.

Sometimes, though, the subject is a bit more complicated. Read these two sentences, all to do with the colour of GOLD, and see if you think they are both correct:

1   To keep the colour YELLOW, copper and silver is added.
2   For RED/PINK gold, the proportion of copper is increased.

The first sentence sounds right, somehow, because copper and silver go together. In fact that sentence is not correct: it should be 'copper and silver *are* added'.

The second sentence is correct: 'the proportion' is the subject, which is singular, and so the verb must be singular – 'is increased' is right.

WHEN THE SUBJECT OF A SENTENCE IS TWO OR MORE
NOUNS, PRONOUNS, ETC JOINED BY *AND*,
THE VERB MUST BE PLURAL

When the subject is two singular nouns joined by 'or'

Here is a third sentence about the colour of GOLD.

3   For WHITE gold, nickel or palladium is added.

In this sentence the person processing the gold has to add *either* nickel (singular) *or* palladium (singular), so the verb has to be singular, – 'is added' is correct.

WHEN THE SUBJECT OF A SENTENCE IS TWO OR MORE
SINGULAR NOUNS, PRONOUNS ETC JOINED BY *OR*,
THE VERB MUST BE SINGULAR

When the subject is two plural nouns joined by 'or'

As you would expect, if the subject is plural, the verb must be plural too, even if the nouns or pronouns are joined by 'or'. So:

'Men or women wait for the train.' is correct. So is 'Cats or dogs are boarded at these kennels.'

But what happens if one part of the subject is singular and the other part is plural, and they are joined by 'or'?

When the subject is a mixture of singular and plural, joined by 'or'

The general rule about this sort of sentence is 'Obey the last order': in other words, the verb agrees with the part of the subject nearest to it. So:

'Two men or *one woman is* usually employed on this job.' is correct. 'Two men or *one woman are* usually employed on this job.' is wrong.

The correct version often sounds a little funny, but logically you can see that it is right.

Finally in this 'and/or' section, let us consider a subject which is written and/or.

When the subject is two nouns joined by 'and/or'

Again the general rule is 'Obey the last order'. So if the second noun is singular, the verb must be singular too.

To go back to the GOLD example, if the last sentence is made technically correct, it should be written:

3 For WHITE gold, nickel and/or palladium is added.

Here is a SUMMARY of the rules you have just studied.

IN SENTENCES WHERE THE SUBJECT IS TWO (OR MORE)
NOUNS OR PRONOUNS ETC
JOINED BY 'AND', 'OR' OR 'AND/OR'

SINGULAR VERB	PLURAL VERB
1 When the joining word is 'or' and both nouns are singular (A man or a woman is employed)	4 When the joining word is 'and' (Men and women are employed)
2 When the joining word is 'or' and the last noun is singular (Two men or a woman is employed)	5 When the joining word is 'or' and the last noun is plural (A man or women are employed)
3 When the joining words are 'and/or' and the last noun is singular (Men and/or a woman is employed)	6 When the joining words are 'and/or' and the last noun is plural (A man and/or women are employed)

Exercise on 'and', 'or' 'and/or'

This is an extract from a summary of a report on the activities of a Personnel Department in a big company

Write or key this extract; whenever you see (is/are), decide whether the verb should be singular (is) or plural (are). The summary table above should help you.

REPORT ON THE PERSONNEL DEPARTMENT
The Report states that both the Personnel and Training functions (is/are) on the same floor in cramped conditions. It recommends that the Personnel or the Training function (is/are) moved to the first floor; it suggests the latter because extra cabinets and/or a cupboard (is/are) available for storing training material. One extra workstation or two desks (is/are) needed for the secretarial support staff.

Check what you wrote. It should have been:

'are' (Example 4 in the summary table)
'is' (Example 1 in the summary table)
'is' (Example 3 in the summary table)
'are' (Example 5 in the summary table)

When the subject sounds plural, but is singular

The rule about a singular subject needing a singular verb still holds good. The problem is that in some sentences a singular verb can sound very odd, so many people, including newsreaders and presenters, say it wrong.

For example, the sentence:

'*A series* of concerts are about to begin.' is *wrong*. Why?

Because the subject is 'A series', which is singular, so the verb should be singular. It should be:

'A *series* of concerts *is* about to begin.'

The problem is even greater when the subject is a long way from the verb. In this sentence, should the missing word be 'is' or 'are'?

'Starting next month, a variety of sitcoms, quiz shows, films and documentaries ? scheduled for Saturday evenings.'

You have to ask yourself what the subject of that sentence is. The answer is 'a variety', which is singular. If the subject is singular, the verb must be singular, so the missing word must be 'is'. Perhaps it sounds funny, but it is right.

Exercise on identifying the subject and verb

All through this chapter so far, you have seen how important it is to identify the exact subject of the sentence. See if you can identify the subject in these sentences: write or key them, putting brackets round the subject and underlining the verb. All the sentences are grammatically correct.

A The Personnel and Training functions both use the Conference Room.
B Whenever the Conference Room is in use, the Personnel or the Training function has to vacate the office next door.
C A series of courses is due to start on Monday of next week.
D Personnel Department secretaries and computer operators are likely to be badly inconvenienced.

■ The verb 'to be'

People quite often muddle up different parts of this verb and put a singular verb with a plural subject; for example, they often say 'we was' or 'I were'.

Below is a table setting out how the verb 'to be' should be said and written in formal English. It is set out in this way because those of you who have learnt a foreign language might be familiar with the layout.

To be

Present tense			
I	am	We	are
You (singular)	are	You (plural)	are
He/she/it	is	They	are
Past tense			
I	was	We	were
You	were	You (plural)	were
He/she/it	was	They	were

If you check on this table, you will see that 'we was', 'he were', 'I be' (found in some dialects) cannot be right.

Note: There is one instance where a construction like 'I were', 'he were' etc is correct; it is when you use a phrase beginning with 'if': 'If I were you, . . .' 'If only she were here, . . .' etc.

Exercise on the verb 'to be'

Use the table if you need to, and every time you see (?), put in the correct form of the verb. Write or key this continuation of the Personnel Department Report; use the PAST tense throughout.

PERSONAL OPINIONS
The opinions of several members of staff (?) sought. In general staff felt happy to work for the Personnel Department, but the following comments (?) made:

'We (?) always having to move.'
'Management did not ask us whether we (?) happy with the new arrangement.'
'I (?) sometimes squashed into a corner, with bad lighting conditions, where it (?) not always convenient to work.'

If you know you sometimes get this verb wrong, use the table to check the correct version.

■ Collective nouns

What is a collective noun?
   A collective noun is one which describes a gathering or collection of things, people or animals. Examples are: a school of dolphins; a murder of crows (yes, that really is right); a flock of sheep. When the collective noun is followed by 'of . . .', it is not difficult to decide that the verb must be singular:

A *school* of dolphins *is* approaching the ship.
A *murder* of crows *was* flying overhead.
A *flock* of sheep *is* in the upper field.

A collective noun can also describe a collection of people without using the word 'of'. Examples are: 'the department', 'the committee', 'the staff', 'management'.

Should the verb in these cases be singular or plural? Should you write or say 'The committee *was* due to meet.' or 'The committee *were* due to meet.'? The answer is, IT DOES NOT MATTER. Either singular or plural is quite acceptable. Strictly speaking it should be singular, because a committee is a singular noun but because a committee is made up of several individuals, people very often use a plural verb. The important thing is to be consistent.

Exercise on collective nouns

We will continue with the Summary of the Report on the Personnel Department. So far you have written about the cramped working conditions, the use of the Conference Room and the personal opinions of members of staff.

This time write or key the following paragraph about attending meetings. Whenever you see something like (was/were), choose the one you think is correct; in each case the singular is shown before the plural. It will always be a verb, and you have to choose whether to make it singular or plural. The secret is to identify the subject which goes with the verb:

- decide whether the subject is singular or plural
- make the verb agree with its subject
- be consistent

MANAGEMENT OF TIME IN THE PERSONNEL DEPARTMENT
It emerged from the Report that a great deal of time (was/were) spent by management attending meetings. The company (requires/require) all management to attend regular communications meetings as well as appropriate committee meetings and appointments. Management (considers/consider) communications meetings to be ineffectual; some even went so far as to say the meetings (was/were) a thorough waste of time.

FOR COLLECTIVE NOUNS SUCH AS DEPARTMENT, COMPANY ETC A SINGULAR OR A PLURAL VERB IS ACCEPTABLE

BE CONSISTENT

■ Personnel/personal

You have now read and written several paragraphs about the Personnel Department, which is the Department in a company which deals with people, their pay, conditions, training, holidays etc.

It is important to remember the difference between PERSONNEL (spelt N–N–E–L at the end of the word) and PERSONAL (spelt N–A–L at the end of the word). PERSONNEL is usually concerned with a lot of people – the Personnel Department or the Company's Personnel (all its employees).

PERSONAL is much more private, concerned with one's own belongings, opinions or feelings.

There are no tricks to help you remember which is which, although the pronunciation does help. PERSON – N – E – L sounds bigger and more open than PERSON – A – L; the bigger word takes the extra 'N'.

Here is a further paragraph under the MANAGEMENT OF TIME IN THE PERSONNEL DEPARTMENT heading. Write or key this paragraph, putting in Personnel or Personal whenever you see (Person?   ).

Some managers queried the need to hold departmental briefing meetings where both (person?   ) and training matters are discussed. A trainer is not concerned, for example, about the safekeeping of (person?   ) belongings and (person?   ) moneys; this is a matter which should be dealt with by the (person?   ) experts.

PERSONNEL IS ABOUT PEOPLE
PERSONAL BELONGS TO YOU

■ Lend/borrow

Many people get 'lend' and 'borrow' mixed up. They say things like 'Can I lend your pen?', which is wrong. It should be 'Can I borrow your pen?'.

It is a question of which way things are going.

A →   →   →   LENDS TO →   →   →   B
A ←   ←   ←   BORROWS FROM ←   ←   ←   B

If you add the words 'to' and 'from' ('lend to' and 'borrow from,') it helps to sort out which word to use.

Sue *lends* her tape *to* Jill
Jill *borrows* the tape *from* Sue

If Sue wants to borrow the tape from Jill, she should say either:

'Can I borrow your tape, please' or
'Can you lend me your tape, please'.
The owner lends. The borrower borrows.

Exercise on lend/borrow

This is the last part of the Summary of the Report on the Personnel Department. Whenever you see [   ] insert either 'lend' or 'borrow'.

SHARED RESOURCES
Personnel Department resources were also a problem. The
Personnel function constantly had to [   ] stationery to the
Training function, which was rarely returned. Conversely, the
Training function had to [   ] secretarial support to the
Personnel function. Personnel frequently had to [   ] from
Training the time and services of the Training Manager's
personal secretary. The Report recommended the pooling of
resources so that neither had to [   ] from the other.
However, shared resources will prove a problem if either the
Training function or the Personnel function is moved to the first
floor (see paragraph 1).

LEND TO
BORROW FROM

Practice

This is part of a Report on the Staff Attitude Survey recently conducted in a large company. Write a summary of this part of the Report in not more than 75 words excluding the heading. You are writing this for the Staff Newsletter; so it needs to be clear and interesting, but factual.

Your summary must contain the following phrases: choose the correct version of the words in brackets.

'The Welsh branches (has/have) not yet been connected'
'Company (person?   )'
'(borrow/lend) staff'
'(Person?) telephone calls'
'Training and practice (is/are) needed'
'Making and/or receiving calls (is/are) . . . . . .'
'The staff (do/does) not abuse the system'.

THE COMPANY'S TELEPHONE SERVICE

Of those who completed the questionnaire 90%, which is a very high percentage, thought that the new telephone equipment was potentially a great asset. However, only 40% thought they were using it to its full capacity. Many members of staff said they did not know what all the buttons did, and some complained they kept cutting other people off when trying to transfer them. It is evident that training in the use of the new equipment is inadequate, and that further practice is required.

The new system has not yet been fully installed in the Welsh branches, so staff in Bangor, Cardiff and Swansea were not able to give their opinion in this part.

When it comes to the service given to customers, 95% thought that making and/or receiving calls formed a large percentage of their workload, but under 50% thought that the service was even adequate. The main faults identified were:

- callers being asked to hang on for too long
- callers being put through to the wrong department
- staff failing to ring back as promised.

The main reasons for these faults were thought to be that shortage of staff and lending personnel to other departments led to undue pressure of work; staff generally were not aware of what other departments required from them, nor of what other departments did.

On the question of personal telephone calls, 82% of those questioned thought that the company ruling on this point was fair, and that the system in general was not abused.

Points to remember from this chapter

- A SINGULAR SUBJECT needs a SINGULAR VERB
  A PLURAL SUBJECT needs a PLURAL VERB
  IDENTIFY YOUR SUBJECT.
- Watch out for sentences in which the subject is words joined by 'and', 'or' or 'and/or'.
- Subjects like 'Committee', 'Department' etc can take either singular or plural, but be consistent.
- 'We was' and 'he/she/it were' are *wrong*.
- 'Personnel' is bigger than 'personal', so takes the extra 'n', followed by 'e'.
- Lend *to*, borrow *from*.

6 Apostrophes Which Show Possession

Learning goals:
- Which word takes the apostrophe?
- Where does the apostrophe go?
- Singular nouns which end in 's'
- Separate
- Where/were

People find apostrophes difficult. Using apostrophes is not so difficult if you think about them carefully. The rules about using apostrophes are very definite (there are no exceptions), so once you have learnt the rules thoroughly, you should be able to use them properly for the rest of your life.

This is the first of three chapters about apostrophes; it deals with the main use of the apostrophe – to show possession. For example in 'the Manager's office', the apostrophe (') shows that the office belongs to the Manager – the Manager 'possesses' the office.

■ Which word takes the apostrophe?

The first thing to do is to identify which word takes the apostrophe. Read these three sentences: each one should have an apostrophe somewhere, but which word needs the apostrophe?

1. Karens anorak is hanging on the right.
2. Samirs anorak is hanging on the left.
3. The childrens anoraks are hanging in the cloakroom.

Ask yourself in each case who the anorak or anoraks belong to (or, to whom the anorak or anoraks belong, which is better grammar).

In sentence 1 the anorak belongs to Karen, in sentence 2 to Samir and in sentence 3 to the children; so 'Karen', 'Samir' and 'children' are the words which need the apostrophes.

You could, in each case, say 'the anorak(s) *of* Karen, Samir or the children' to establish who owns something (in this case a garment).

Exercise in identifying which word takes the apostrophe

Write or key these five sentences. In each case underline or embolden the word you think should have the apostrophe. Do not at this stage worry about where the apostrophe should be. Ask yourself who or what owns something; if you can say, in sentence 4, 'the job of a leader', it must be the leader who owns the job, and therefore the leader who needs the apostrophe.

4   A leaders job is to supervise the children.
5   The childrens toys are kept in separate boxes.
6   Flags and bunting are used to decorate the schools main room.
7   The girls changing area is separate from the boys changing area.
8   Parents are encouraged to ask the teachers opinion.

In sentence 4, as you know, you should have underlined or emboldened A leader, because the job belongs to the leader (the leader owns the job).

In sentence 5, you should have underlined or emboldened the children, because the children own the toys.

In sentence 6, it should have been the school; we are talking about the main room of the school.

In sentence 7, we are talking about the changing area *of* the girls and the boys, so you should have underlined or emboldened both girls and boys.

In sentence 8, the teacher (or teachers) have or own the opinion.

■ Where does the apostrophe go?

Once you have identified which word should have the apostrophe, you can decide where the apostrophe should go – before or after the s.

AN APOSTROPHE IS **ALWAYS** BEFORE OR AFTER
AT LEAST ONE 'S'

Look again at the eight sentences about the Nursery School; we will treat each one separately. The easiest way to decide where to put the apostrophe is to decide what the word would be *without* the apostrophe, and put the apostrophe at the end of the basic word. Then add an 's' if it is needed.

Sentence 1 "Karens anorak is hanging on the right."
- The anorak belongs to Karen
- Karen is the basic word
- Put the apostrophe at the end of the basic word (Karen)
- Add an 's' if needed (Karen's)
"Karen's anorak is hanging on the right."

Sentence 2 "Samirs anorak is hanging on the left."
- The anorak belongs to Samir
- Samir is the basic word
- Put the apostrophe at the end of the basic word (Samir)
- Add an 's' if needed (Samir's)
"Samir's anorak is hanging on the left."

Sentence 3 "The childrens anoraks are hanging in the cloakroom."
- The anoraks belong to whom?
- What is, therefore, the basic word?
- Put the apostrophe at the end of the basic word (children)
- Add an 's' if needed (children's)
"The children's anoraks are hanging in the cloakroom."

Sentence 4 "A leaders job is to supervise the children."
- The job belongs to whom?
- What is the basic word?
- Put the apostrophe at the end of the basic word (leader)
- Add an 's' if needed (leader's)
"A leader's job is to supervise the children."

Sentence 5 "The childrens toys are kept in separate boxes."
- What is the basic word (to whom do the toys belong?)?
- Add an apostrophe to the end of the basic word and add the 's' if needed (children's)

"The children's toys are kept in separate boxes."

Sentence 6 "Flags and bunting are used to decorate the schools main room."
- The basic word is ?
- Add an apostrophe and an 's' if needed

"Flags and bunting are used to decorate the school's main room."

Sentence 7 "The girls changing area is separate from the boys changing area."
- Which are the basic words – to whom does each separate changing area belong?
- The basic words must be girls and boys (both plural)
- Add the apostrophe to the end of the basic word - girls' and boys'
- Because you already have an 's' to make each word plural, you do not need to add another 's' – leave it as girls' and boys'

"The girls' changing area is separate from the boys' changing area."

Sentence 8 "Parents are encouraged to ask the teachers opinion."
- What is the basic word? To whom does the opinion belong? It could be one teacher or several teachers. You have to decide whether, from the context, it is more likely to be the opinion of one teacher or several teachers.
- If you decide it is *only one* teacher, then teacher is the basic word. Add the apostrophe and an 's' if needed, and you get teacher's.
- If you decide it is the opinion of *more than one* teacher (of two or three teachers), then teachers (plural) is the basic word. Add the apostrophe (teachers'). Because you already have an 's' to make the word plural you do not need to add another.

For one teacher (SINGULAR)
'Parents are encouraged to ask the teacher's opinion.'
For two or more teachers (PLURAL)
'Parents are encouraged to ask the teachers' opinion.'

WHAT IS THE BASIC WORD?
ADD THE APOSTROPHE
ADD AN 'S' IF NECESSARY

Exercise on inserting the apostrophe

Write or key this paragraph, inserting an apostrophe in the correct place in each emboldened word.

The **schools** opening times are from 9.00 am to 12.00 noon. There is one break at 10.30 am, when the children are given milk or juice and biscuits; **parents** wishes about diet are taken into consideration.

The children are divided into groups by age; each **groups** leader is a fully trained nursery school teacher. Girls and boys are not separated for the different activities, but naturally the **girls** and **boys** toilet facilities are separate.

The apostrophes should have been before the 's' in school's (basic word 'school'); after the 's' in parents' (basic word 'parents' – no need to add another 's' where the word is plural and already has an 's'); before the 's' in group's (basic word 'group'); after the 's' in girls', and boys' (basic words 'girls' and 'boys').

IDENTIFY THE BASIC WORD
ADD THE APOSTROPHE
ADD AN 'S' IF NECESSARY

■ Singular nouns which end in 's'

What do you do about a singular noun which ends in 's', or even 'ss'? Names like James and Francis or Frances come into this category; so do nouns like dress or crisis. The same rules apply but sometimes people add another 's' after the apostrophe, so you get words like James's, Francis's, Frances's, dress's (3 sss!) or crisis's.

Here are some example sentences:

Francis' work is done *or*   The dress' hem is down *or*
Francis's work is done.   The dress's hem is down.

Either is correct; it depends which looks or sounds better. With James it is usual to put in the extra 's'. You will usually see St James's Park, because that is the way you tend to say it.

The rule for singular nouns which end in 's' is:

IDENTIFY THE BASIC WORD
ADD THE APOSTROPHE
ADD AN EXTRA 'S' IF YOU THINK IT SOUNDS OR LOOKS
BETTER, BUT IT IS ACCEPTABLE WITHOUT THE EXTRA 'S'

Note: People use fewer apostrophes these days. In written English always use the apostrophe if it will help the reader.

■ Separate

You will probably have noticed that the word 'separate', 'separately' or 'separated' has been used several times in this chapter. This is one of the words frequently mis-spelt. People write seperate, which is wrong.

To help you remember this, think of what the word 'separate' means – to keep apart. As you can see, se*par*ate and a*par*t both have p-a-r in the middle.

SE*PAR*ATE = A*PAR*T

■ Where/were

In some dialects (Liverpudlian, for example) these two words are pronounced in much the same way, which makes it difficult to remember which is which and whether the word should have an 'h' or not.

Where   (with an 'h') is to do with a place – 'here' or 'there'. Both 'here' and 'there' have an 'h', which might help you to remember.

Were   (without an 'h') is part of the verb 'to be', as we saw in the previous chapter. There is no 'h' in any part of this verb.

I am	We are	I was	We were
You are	You are	You were	You were
He/she/it is	They are	He/she/it was	They were

so do not put an 'h' in 'were'.

Exercise on separate and where/were

Write, type or word process this paragraph. Every time you see (where/were) choose the correct word; every time you see sep?rate put in the correct vowel.

(Where/were) do you buy your clothes? Some people prefer to shop in the Sep?rates Department of the big Department Stores. Others shop in the smaller shops. Last time you (where/were) doing some clothes shopping, which did you do? Did you go with your friend, or did you shop sep?rately? (Where/were) you able to find what you wanted?

Remember separate = apart.

The first (where/were) should be where, because it is to do with a place – could be here or there. The second should be were, and so should the third. They are both to do with what you are doing or being – ie, part of the verb.

Practice

You are working in the Reception Department of a busy hotel, taking lots of telephone messages, which you have to write or key.

These are the messages. They contain some words which need possessive apostrophes, some uses of sep?rate and some instances of (where/were).

Message 1 to Reservations Clerk
Mrs B Brown needs to know whether she can book a sep?rate room for her two children, aged 10 and 9. Please ring her back.

Message 2 to Reception
Mr C Astley rang to ask if he can park his car near (where/were) his room is situated. He has some very heavy luggage and his wifes disability prevents her from walking too far. I said we would make sure he could.

Message 3 to Banqueting Manager

Chef wanted to know when you (where/were) expecting the party of 10 to arrive. They arrived earlier than he thought, which put all the waiters timings out and the starters were not ready. Please give him a ring.

Message 4 to Reception

Mr and Mrs James have left their passports in the safe. Please could you leave Mr James passport out ready for him at 8.30 tomorrow morning.

Message 5 to the Deputy Manager

The Housekeeper rang to say that Room Nos 24 and 25 (where/were) still occupied after 12.00 noon. Do you want the guests billed sep?rately for the extra time? Please let Reception know.

Message 6 to the Manager

The staff car park is very full because of the building work. Please could you let Reception know if staff can be permitted to park in the guests car park for the next two days.

Points to remember from this chapter

- POSSESSIVE APOSTROPHES:
    - Identify which word needs the apostrophe
    - What is the basic word?
    - Add the apostrophe to the end of the basic word
    - Add an 's' if necessary
- Singular nouns which end in 's' sometimes need an extra 's' if it sounds or looks better
- Separate = apart
- Where is to do with place (here or there)
  Were is part of the verb to be

Kenton Library
Issue Receipt

Customer name: Mr Jack Barlow Sakhe
Customer ID: ****8588

Title: English language skills
ID: C285264800
Due: 06/07/17

Total items: 1
08/06/2017 12:35
Checked out: 1
Overdue: 0
Hold requests: 0
Ready for pickup: 0

Thank you for using Newcastle Libraries.

7 Apostrophes Which Show Omitted Letters

Learning goals:
- How and when to use the omission apostrophe
- When to use omission apostrophes in business
- When to use 'more' or '- - - - - er'
- Whether/weather

The second use of the apostrophe (') is to show when some letters have been left out of a word, particularly when two words have been run together, like let's (let us), can't (can not) etc.

■ How and when to use the omission apostrophe

Where to insert the apostrophe

This apostrophe is very easy to use. You simply put in an apostrophe when something has been left out of the middle of a word, or of two words run together. The word is abbreviated (made shorter) in this way.

It does not matter how many letters are missing – you use only one apostrophe, wherever something is left out. For example:

let's is short for let us
the apostrophe comes between the 't' and the 's'
to take the place of the missing 'u'

Do the same for these words:

cant   dont   couldnt   shouldnt

There are some exceptions to the general rule:

1 Shan't is short for shall not, but we write it with only one apostrophe – shan't – to take the place of the missing 'o'. Strictly speaking it should be written sha'n't to show the missing 'lls' as well.
2 Fish n' chips is often written like that; it should really be fish 'n' chips to show that both the 'a' and the 'd' are missing.
3 Won't is an odd word. It is short for will not, of course, and the apostrophe shows the missing 'o' (as in shan't). In won't the vowel has changed as well, because it would be very difficult to say willn't or win't.

Why words are written in this way

The main reason for writing words like this is to show how they are said in informal, everyday conversation. You are unlikely to say could not, cannot, do not etc, unless you want to emphasise the word or words in sentences like:

'I really do not like nuts.'
'I simply could not bring myself to do it.'

Another reason for shortening a word by using an apostrophe is when the word is too long to fit in a given space (a computer field, perhaps). If you watch football results on television on a Saturday afternoon, you will sometimes see names like Middlesbrough written as M'brough.

These are ways of shortening, or abbreviating the words, but they are not true abbreviations like ad or advert for advertisement, or exam for examination. Words like advert and exam are really a short form of quite a long word, and you will notice that the whole of the end of the word (not the middle) is omitted. Apostrophes are used when something is left out in the middle of a word or short phrase.

Exercise on inserting omission apostrophes

In these paragraphs from a Sunday newspaper report of an interrupted tennis match, insert the apostrophes which show where a letter or letters have been left out.

> The players were forced to abandon the match at the end of the first set because of rain. Cooper said he hadnt really got into the match at that stage – the score of 6-0 to Rowden confirms this.
>
> Cooper couldnt get his first service to work at all, and towards the end of the set didnt seem to have the heart to continue. Rowden followed up his powerful service throughout with accurate net play and ground shots which swung and dipped over the net. Play in this match wont be resumed until Monday afternoon.

■ When to use omission apostrophes in business

Most business written work will not, or should not, contain words like isn't, didn't, or I'm, although a few business letters between colleagues who know each other well do follow that style. For most purposes it is far safer to assume you must never use these sorts of words in formal business documents.

There are exceptions, of course. The main exceptions are:

- E-mail
- Very informal, chatty letters you receive from companies trying to sell you something (promotional letters)
- Advertisements
- Newspapers and magazines
- Scripts for videos, commercials etc

You will see that this is a list of very specialised business English, some of which you will be studying in Chapters 9 and 13. In this chapter we will look briefly at promotional letters.

Exercise on using words with omission apostrophes

This is the opening paragraph of a promotional letter trying to sell you some prestige luggage. Write or key it. As you do, put omission apostrophes in to shorten the **emboldened** words or phrases.

> Dear Customer
> When you last went on holiday, were you happy with your luggage?
> **Did not** you look round and think to yourself, '**They are** smart, those bags over there'? Look now at this beautiful set of luggage on the page opposite. **Is not it** elegant? And it could be yours for only £99.99. **I am** sure you will not be able to resist it when I tell you **it is** made from real hide and comes in subtle shades of brown and grey.

Check what you have written with the version on page **??**. Note particularly the abbreviation of 'They are'.

■ When to use 'more' or '- - - -er'

It is not right to use both 'more *and* '- - - -er' when you want to say something is more whatever it is than something else. You have to say either, for example, *more* strong *or* stronger. To say that "Nylon is more stronger than wool" is grammatically *wrong*. You must say either "Nylon is stronger than wool." or "Nylon is more strong than wool."

This rule has no exceptions: to use both '- - - -er' and 'more' is *wrong*.

There is no absolute rule about whether to use '- - - -er' or 'more'. Generally speaking you use '- - - -er' when the word is a short, everyday sort of word such as:

weak, hard, short, soft,
strong, easy, long, tough.

You use 'more' for the longer, more unusual words such as:

unusual, beautiful, fantastic,
difficult, realistic, wonderful.

They are all adjectives, as you can see.

Exercise on 'more' or '- - - - er'

Add a further paragraph to the 'luggage' letter; write or key it and as you do so:

- insert the omission apostrophes needed in the emboldened words.
- whenever you see an adjective in brackets, make it comparative by adding either 'more' or '- - - -er'.

To make this offer even (exciting), **we are** offering you a free entry in our GRAND PRIZE DRAW if your Order Form is received within 10 working days. It **could not** be (easy). Just post off your Order Form TODAY. And **do not** forget that this beautiful luggage is made from real leather, which is (elegant) and (strong) than plastic.

■ Whether/weather

Very few people actually pronounce the 'h' in 'whether', any more than they do in words like 'which', 'what' or 'why'. If they did, it would be easier for them to remember to spell the word with an 'h'.

The word 'whether' means 'if', or course. 'Weather' (minus an 'h' and plus an 'a') is about the rain, sun, snow, fog and everything else that goes to make up our unpredictable climate.

The sentence 'I wonder whether the weather will be fine.' might help you to remember which is which.

Exercise on whether/weather

Add a final paragraph to the luggage letter.

1　Insert the omission apostrophes in the emboldened words.
2　Add 'more' or '- - - -er', as you did before.
3　Where you see w- - - - - -, insert whether or weather(s).

For a truly superb addition to your travelling wardrobe, which will stay looking good in all w- - - - - -, you **will not** be able to resist our unbeatable price. Remember **it is** only £99.99. W- - - - - - **you are** travelling in the UK or abroad, you will arrive looking (smart) and (confident) than you have ever done before. ACT NOW and send off your Order TODAY!

Check the whole letter now against this version.

Dear Customer

When you last went on holiday, were you happy with your luggage? Didn't you look around and think to yourself 'They're smart, those bags over there!'? Look now at this beautiful set of luggage on the page opposite. Isn't it elegant? And it could be yours for only £99.99. I'm sure you won't be able to resist it when I tell you it's made from real hide and comes in subtle shades of brown and grey.

To make this offer even more exciting, we're offering you a free entry in our GRAND PRIZE DRAW if your Order Form is received within 10 working days. It couldn't be easier. Just post off your Order Form TODAY. And don't forget that this beautiful luggage is made from real leather, which is more elegant and stronger than plastic.

For a truly superb addition to your travelling wardrobe, which will stay looking good in all weathers, you won't be able to resist our unbeatable price. Remember, it's yours for only £99.99. Whether you're travelling in the UK or abroad, you'll arrive looking smarter and more confident than you've ever done before. ACT NOW and send off your Order TODAY!
Yours sincerely

Note especially:

'They're for 'they are'	'you're for 'you are'
'it's' for 'it is'	'you've for 'you have'.

These are all abbreviations or contractions, so each needs an omission apostrophe.

Practice

Choose something that you might be likely to buy from a catalogue or by mail order, and write your own chatty promotional letter, setting out all its good points and trying to persuade unknown customers that it is just the thing for them. It can be jewellery, sportswear, household equipment, hi-fi – anything you like.

As you write your letter please do the following:

- Have one idea for each sentence. Do not use a comma to separate ideas; use a full stop and start a new sentence.
- Keep the sentences reasonably short.
- Each paragraph should be about one topic.
- Use abbreviated words such as won't, can't etc, which include omission apostrophes.
- Make sure you use at least one adjective which takes 'more' (eg more hardwearing), and one which takes '- - -er' (eg cheaper).
- Try to use the word 'whether', and 'weather' as well, if you can squeeze it in.
- Make sure your letter is well presented, with good margins.

Points to remember from this chapter

- Omission apostrophes show that something has been left out – eg it's for it is; you've for you have; you're for you are and they're for they are.
- Do not use omission apostrophes in formal, written English.
- You can use them in informal letters, e-mail, advertisements etc.
- More smaller is wrong. Use either 'more' or '- - - -er' but not both.
- I wonder whether the weather will be fine.

8 Its and Their

Learning goals:
- Its and it's
- There, their and they're
- Apostrophes in plurals
- Did/done

This is the last chapter on apostrophes. The two previous chapters have explained how possessive apostrophes and omission apostrophes should be used. This chapter emphasises when you should *not* use an apostrophe.

■ Its and it's

As you saw in the previous chapter, **it's** is an abbreviation or contraction for 'it is', so should not be used in formal written English. **Its** shows that something belongs to it, as my, your, his etc do. Look at the following table, and you will see how 'its' fits into this pattern.

My	Our
Your (singular)	Your (plural)
His/her/its	Their

None of these words takes an apostrophe

Read these two rather long sentences from a Memo about the installation of a computer network:

'*My* own view is that *your* Memo should have been sent to John to get *his* input on the design, to Jane for *her* opinion on the costings and to the Personnel Department for *its* thoughts on the training.

We could have put forward *our* combined recommendations to you and Alwyn for *your* consideration; you could then have forwarded it to the client's Directors for *their* decision.'

You can see that 'its' takes its natural place, without an apostrophe, among my, your, his etc.

Exercise on its and it's

Write or key this Memo; make sure that 'its' is correctly written – with or without an apostrophe – throughout.

To: WINSTON HEWSON   Ref: SH/VC
        Systems Analyst

From: SUE HAMPSON   Date:
        Project Manager

M & P HOOK LTD – INSTALLATION OF COMPUTER NETWORK

Your Memo of yesterday is to hand. I have, in fact, already asked John for his final designs and Jane for the revised costings. The Personnel Department is talking direct to the clients about **its** training recommendations. The network is due to be installed at the end of next month; as you know, **its** prompt delivery is vital to our good relations with this particular client. Please let me have your own timetable for testing the software as soon as possible. It is most important that we put this package together with speed and efficiency.

Note that 'It is', which starts the last sentence, is written out in full, because this is a formal Memo, and the words should not be shortened to 'it's'. The other two instances of 'its' are like 'his', 'her' and 'your', so do not need an apostrophe.

■ There, their and they're

You saw in the previous chapter that 'they're' is short for 'they are', so should not, generally speaking, be used in formal business English. 'Their' and 'there' are used, of course, and people frequently muddle them up.

When we were thinking about how to spell 'where' and 'were' in Chapter 6, we suggested that you think of where as something to do with place. "Where is it? There!" The spellings are similar. Now you can do the same the other way round and remember:

THERE IS TO DO WITH PLACE. WHERE? THERE

You use 'there' in phrases like 'there is' or 'there are' as well, but in a sense that is still to do with place.

THEIR is linked up with my, your, its, our etc. Here is the table again, to remind you.

My	Our
Your (singular)	Your (plural)
His/her/its	Their

Exercise on their/there

Winston Hewson replies to Sue Hampson's Memo about the installation of the computer network. Write or key this Memo; use the same reference and heading.

Whenever you see their/there, make sure you use the correct word.

Thank you for yesterday's Memo. I enclose my suggestions for testing the software on the client's premises. I think they have been having trouble with their/there power supply, so it is better to test it their/there than at our own offices.

Their/there is one other matter I should like to mention: I hope the training is being organised for small groups rather than one large one. Their/there are several points which will require individual attention.

I was pleased to talk to you on the telephone this morning. Their/there is no doubt that our conversation helped to clear up any misunderstanding.

Check that your work is totally correct. The first time you used the word, it should have been 'their' because it is the power supply which belongs to them; every other time you should have used 'there'. Note that 'they have' in the first paragraph is written out in full.

■ Apostrophes in plurals

In most cases we can say quite definitely:

DO NOT USE AN APOSTROPHE TO MAKE A SIMPLE PLURAL

To write or say something like "This shop sells purses', handbags', wallets' and briefcases' " is definitely *wrong*. These are simple plurals like tables, chairs, cabbages and kings. They do *not* need an apostrophe.

On some rare occasions you might want to use an apostrophe to show a plural, but only when it helps to make the meaning clear. You can use it, for example, when you are using figures or single letters, and you want to write them in the plural. Some examples are:

- They came in 2's and 3's.
- Mind your P's and Q's.
- This company started in the 1920's.

As you can see, an apostrophe is correctly used in plurals in very special cases. It would be quite all right to use these words without the apostrophe anyway – eg 2s and 3s, Ps and Qs, 1920s. So it is almost 100% safe to say:

DO NOT USE AN APOSTROPHE TO MAKE A SIMPLE PLURAL

Exercise on apostrophes in plurals

The exchange of Memos between Winston Hewson and Sue Hampson continues. Write or key this Memo from Sue to Winston, using the same headings. Insert any apostrophes which you think should be added. Do the same as in the previous Memo for their/there.

Thank you for your suggestions for testing the software. I agree that this should be done on the client's premises, and have informed them accordingly. Their/there Managing Director will be coming into the office on Friday. We will make final arrangements then. Can you attend a meeting at 1030 please?

The training is scheduled for small groups. Bob Weller from our own Training Department will train all the client's personnel in 2s and 3s.

I am confident that the package we are providing will suit our client, and should take them well into the 2000s. They seem very happy with the software programs so far. Are their/there any plans for upgrading the software in the next three years or so? Although the program is comprehensive now, its data processing facility might become over-utilised and need further capacity.

Perhaps you could let me know what you think before the meeting on Friday.

Please check your work. You did not need to add any apostrophes at all, but it would have been quite correct if you had written 2's, 3's and 2000's. 'Its' definitely does not need an apostrophe, because it is not an abbreviation of 'it is'. The first time their/there appeared, you should have used 'their' (the Managing Director belonging to them), and the second time you should have used 'there'.

■ Did/done

Do you sometimes hear people say "He done it" or "I done it"? They are wrong. It should always be 'He did', 'I did', as you can see from this chart:

I did	We did
You did	You did
He/she/it did	They did

People who get this wrong are probably muddling it up with 'I have done' or 'he has done'.

I have done	We have done
You have done	You have done
He/she/it has done	They have done

This rule has no exceptions. You should never write or say 'Who done it?' It should be 'Who did it?' because 'done' goes with has or have.

The only time you should ever use 'done' without 'have' or 'has' is when you are talking about a 'whodunnit' (a detective novel), and then it is spelt differently (and wrong!) as you can see.

Exercise on did/done

We have come to the final Memo in this series. The two memo senders are much more friendly than they were at the beginning of the exchange, and the tone of this Memo reflects this fact.

Once again write or key the Memo. This time there are sometimes mistakes in the use of it's/its, their/there and apostrophes in plurals. Did/done is also used incorrectly. As you work through the Memo, think carefully about each occasion when these words are used; if you think that what is written is wrong, correct it. Use the same headings and reference as before.

Thank you for your latest Memo. It's very encouraging to hear that the clients are pleased with the software. Their requirements are very unusual – I am glad we seem to have met them.

I shall be pleased to attend the meeting at 10.00 am on Friday. Are their any more papers you would like me to bring? I have already done a plan for updating the software in 2005. I can bring this with me to the meeting if you wish. Have you any idea who done the original plan? I joined the company after it had been started, as you know.

Thank you for letting me know about the training schedules. I have let Bob have a copy of the network system and its accompanying documentation.

I am looking forward to the meeting on Friday, and will make sure I am there promptly.

Best of luck!

Check your work: working backwards – 'there' in the last sentence is correct; 'its' in the previous sentence is also correct; 'who done the original plan' is wrong – it should have been 'did'; 'I have already done' is right. 'Are their any more papers?' is wrong, but 'their requirements' is right. 'It's' (It is) in the second sentence is alright, because this Memo is more friendly, and the tone has changed.

Practice

Read this extract from a Report on a computer network. Try to take note of all the apostrophes and the use of its, their and there.

IN-HOUSE COMPUTER NETWORK

The network was finally up and running in January 2002, one month behind schedule. Its installation took longer than anticipated and there were some bugs in the software. The suppliers assured us that these were normal teething troubles and that there should be no further problems once the system was properly used.

The suppliers' training department undertook the training of all our personnel. The training was completed in time, although their training material was not as tailor-made as we would have wished. The trainers seemed to be using exercises designed for a system slightly different from ours, which confused some of the operators.

The system has now been working reasonably well for nearly twelve months. Its shortcomings are:

- Slow response time for e-mail.
- Inadequate number of terminals, due to expansion.
- A certain amount of data falling off the system.
- Very slow response time when printing out graphics and all terminals are in use.

The suppliers have pointed out that the network's capacity is already being over-stretched – hence the slow response time and loss of data. If further terminals are added, this will exacerbate the problem unless the software is upgraded and the memory increased. Their Systems Analyst has submitted plans to meet these two requirements.

Answer these questions: your answers must be complete sentences in your own words. Take particular care with all the topics studied in this chapter.

1 Why was the installation of the network completed one month behind schedule?
2 How could the suppliers' training department have improved the service to their client?
3 Although the system has been running reasonably well, it has certain shortcomings. Which of these was due to an increase in personnel, rather than a fault in the system itself?

4   The suppliers' Systems Analyst has submitted plans to overcome these difficulties. What were his two main recommendations?

Points to remember from this chapter

-   Do not use it's or they're in formal written English.
-   There - where?
-   Their is like our, your, his, her and its.
-   DO NOT USE APOSTROPHES TO MAKE SIMPLE PLURALS.
-   'She done it' is *wrong*. It should be 'She has done it' or 'She did it'.

9 Quotation Marks

Learning goals:
- Using double quotation marks
- Using single quotation marks
- Common phrases – separate or together?
- Sight/site

Whether to use single quotation marks or double quotation marks (inverted commas) is sometimes a matter of opinion. The only firm rule is to BE CONSISTENT.

One method is to use double quotes for actual speech and single quotes for showing what someone else has said or written; but it could be the other way round!

This chapter will set out how to use double quotes and the punctuation needed for direct speech (dialogue); single quotes will be used for quoting from what people have said or written, and to highlight certain words.

■ Using double quotation marks

When you read a book, you will see that what is actually said has quotation marks before and after it. You might see some something like:

> "Don't forget," he reminded her, "be there at 8.00."
> She snapped back, "You know I'll be there." And then she said, "Is Phil coming?"
> "Yes, of course," he replied. "He always does."

Let us analyse the punctuation to establish the rules.

"Don't forget," he reminded her, *"be there at 8.00."*

"Don't forget,"
Somebody is actually saying 'Don't forget' so there must be quotation marks round these words. The first word 'Don't' starts the sentence, so needs a capital letter. There is a comma after 'forget' because it is accepted practice to put a comma before the quotation marks if the speech is followed by something like 'he said', 'he reminded her'.

he reminded her,
This phrase is not actually said, so is outside the quotation marks. The whole spoken sentence is not yet finished, so there is a comma after 'her' .

"be there at 8.00."
These words are spoken, so they need quotation marks. The spoken sentence is now complete, so it needs a full stop.

She snapped back, "You know I'll be there."

She snapped back, These words are not spoken, so do not need quotes. They do need a comma, because she is going on to say something.

"You know I'll be there." Speech needs quotes. What she says is a sentence, so must start with a capital letter.

And then she said, "Is Phil coming?"
This sentence is similar to the previous one.

And then she said,
No quotes, but a comma before the quotation marks.

"Is Phil coming?"
Quotes, *capital letter for the first word* because it is the start of a sentence. Question mark instead of a full stop.

"Yes, of course," he replied. "He always does."

"Yes, of course," he replied.
Quotation marks are used for the speech, and the last thing before the closing quotes is a comma, because it is going to be followed by 'he replied'. Do not use a full stop here, but do use a question mark or an exclamation mark if what is said requires one.

"He always does."
Quotation marks are used, the sentence starts with a capital letter and ends with a full stop because there is nothing following.

START A NEW LINE FOR EACH PERSON WHO SPEAKS

The general rules for using punctuation in dialogue in a book, an article or something similar are as follows. (Please note that quotation marks are not used in scripts for plays, videos etc. The layout is quite different, as we shall see in Chapter 13.)

1 PUT IN QUOTATION MARKS ANYTHING ACTUALLY SAID.
2 ALWAYS START THE SPOKEN SENTENCE WITH A CAPITAL LETTER, EVEN IF IT COMES AFTER SOMETHING LIKE 'HE SAID'. (. . . she said, "Is Phil coming?")
3 BEFORE THE CLOSING QUOTATION MARKS:
   - USE A COMMA IF 'HE SAID' ETC FOLLOWS (". . of course," he replied) EXCEPT WHEN THE SPOKEN WORDS NEED A QUESTION MARK OR AN EXCLAMATION MARK. ("Don't!" he shouted.)
   - USE A FULL STOP AT THE END OF A SENTENCE IF NOTHING FOLLOWS. ("He always does.")
4 WHEN A SENTENCE OF SPOKEN WORDS IS BROKEN BY 'HE SAID', ETC, USE A COMMA AT THE END OF THE FIRST HALF OF THE SENTENCE AND START THE SECOND HALF WITH A SMALL LETTER. ("Don't forget," he reminded her, "be there at 8.00.")
5 START A NEW LINE FOR EACH PERSON WHO SPEAKS.

The point which most people forget, if they do get their punctuation wrong, is No 2: always start what is said with a capital letter.

Exercise on double quotation marks

It is not very often that you will be asked to write or key dialogue in the business world, although it is sometimes required in exams.

One instance where it is used is setting up a scenario for a training session. People who attend training courses often have to do case studies: they discuss and comment on a scene that they read, and this scene sometimes contains dialogue.

The following is the beginning of a scene set in a supermarket.

It has dialogue which has no punctuation. Write, type or word process the whole scene with the correct quotation marks and other punctuation.

Mr Kallen, the manager, was walking past the delicatessen counter. He noticed the good display and the clean dishes, but he also noticed that the price tickets were dirty and cracked.
Straighten your tickets he barked
What came the startled reply
Mr Kallen barked again straighten your tickets and make sure they're clean
Yes OK said the Sales Assistant feeling fed up about the whole thing when I've served this customer

Check your work: you can see how difficult it is to read without the punctuation. In particular check the dialogue with this version:

"Straighten your tickets," he barked.
"What?" came the startled reply.
Mr Kallen barked again, "Straighten your tickets, and make sure they're clean."
"Yes, OK," said the Sales Assistant, feeling fed up about the whole thing, "when I've served this customer."

■ Using single quotation marks

Single quotation marks are used:

- To show that the writer is quoting from what someone else has said or written. Remember that some people use double quotation marks for this. It does not matter which you use, provided you are consistent.
- To highlight a word, often because it is a bit unusual or is technical.
- To separate a word from the rest of the sentence, so that it is easier to read.

Single quotation marks used to show a quote

In his Annual Report to shareholders, the Chairman stressed that security, which had been a problem during the previous year, was now under much better control. He emphasised that 'staff vigilance is of prime importance' in keeping thefts to a minimum.

In this extract from a report on an Annual General Meeting, the writer has quoted the Chairman's actual words, and has put them in single quotation marks to show this. Notice that no extra punctuation marks are needed. The writer has only to put quotation marks round the words actually quoted.

Single quotation marks used to highlight a word

He went on to say that 'shrinkage' has also been reduced, so that profits had been increased.

'Shrinkage' is a technical word which readers of the report on this meeting might find unusual, so the writer has put it in single quotes. It means losses which cannot easily be identified, like stock which is damaged or out-of-date and cannot be sold, and for which a credit has not been claimed.

Again all the writer needs to do is put quotation marks round the word, with no extra punctuation.

Single quotation marks used to make a sentence easier to read

All punctuation is to help the reader, and sometimes it is helpful to put a word in single quotes. It makes the reader pause for a fraction of a second because the word in quotes stands out from the other words. Read this sentence aloud:

When you are filing in alphabetical order, ignore the word 'the' and file under the first letter of the next word.

If the writer had not used single quotes round the word 'the' it would have made the sentence much more difficult to read. Try reading this aloud:

You should use an instead of a when the next words starts with a vowel.

It would be much easier to read if 'an' and 'a' were in quotation marks.

Exercise on single quotation marks

This is part of a speech made by someone who is very concerned about the litter in the local park. Write or key it, putting in single quotation marks wherever there is:

- a direct quote
- an unusual word
- a word which needs quotes to make the sentence clear.

The Residents' Association has carried out a survey of all our local parks and gardens. They say that, and I quote, the litter in Queen's Gardens just off the High Street is particularly bad.

Ladies and gentlemen, I am sure the time has come to press our Council to do something about these litterbugs, as we used to call them. And I use the word our deliberately. It is our elected Council, and they must be made to see that the litter problem is ruining our town.

When a speaker is making a speech, it is very important that he or she can read it easily; the correct use of quotation marks will help him or her to do so.

In this speech, you should have put quotes round 'the litter in the Queen's Gardens just off the High Street is particularly bad', because it is a straight quote from the Residents' Association's survey. You might have put quotes round 'litterbugs', because it is an unusual word. You should have put quotes around 'our' in the phrase 'I use the word 'our' deliberately'; it makes the sentence much easier to read. You could have put quotes round the second 'our' as well ('our' elected Council) because the speaker wanted to highlight that word.

There are three other things to remind you about in these two paragraphs, and one which will be dealt with in more detail later in the book.

- The Residents' Association takes an apostrophe after the 's'. The basic word is Residents (the Association belongs to the Residents). Put the apostrophe at the end of the basic word. In this case there is no need to add another 's', because it would sound very ugly. (Possessive apostrophes are dealt with in Chapter 6.)

- 'and I quote' is a sub-clause, so needs a pair of commas round it. (See Chapter 2.)
- The extract is divided into two paragraphs, because the topic for each is different. The first paragraph could be headed 'Residents' Association Survey' and the second 'Approach to the Council'. (Paragraphs are dealt with in Chapter 1.)
- The quotation mark at the end of the actual quote from the survey goes immediately after the quote has finished and before the full stop. '. . . . . is particularly bad'. (Similar rules about where the full stop should go when you use brackets are given in Chapter 11.)

■ Common phrases – separate or together?

Some people have difficulty in deciding whether to run certain words together. Here are some common phrases which are sometimes written incorrectly. You can use this table as a reference when you come to use the phrases.

✓	X
RIGHT	*WRONG*
a lot of	alot of
in fact	infact
and so	andso
on account of	onaccount of
thank you for your letter	thankyou for your letter
all right; alright*	allright
on top of	ontop of

*Alright is one of those spellings that some people still consider incorrect; they say that things are 'all right' or 'all wrong'. However, the spelling 'alright' is now so commonly used that you would not be penalised for writing it that way.

What muddles people, perhaps, are the phrases you see and hear on the television like 'Loads a money' or 'Lotta bottle'. These are catchphrases you might use when talking to your friends; they are not acceptable in formal written English.

There is no exercise for these phrases, but you will be asked to use some of them in the Practice section of this chapter.

■ Sight/site

This is another pair or words which confuses people. There is no easy way of remembering which is which.

SIGHT is to do with eyes and seeing
SITE is to do with a place or location (This is IT)

Phrases in which you should use *sight*; they are all to do with seeing:

Her eyesight was getting worse
A sight for sore eyes
With hindsight
You look a sight
May I have sight of the document, please

To go sight-seeing
To see the sights
To know someone by sight
Sight and sound

Phrases in which you should use *site*; they are all to do with places.

A building site
An excavation site
On site

A site for the new factory
A camping site (See chapter 2.)

THIS IS *IT!*

Exercise on sight/site

Write or key this letter. Whenever you see sight/site, choose the correct word; the list above should help you.

(Date)

Mr P Green
Green & Grey Buildings Ltd
102 Lambton Way
CARLISLE
CA3 2FX

Dear Mr Green

67 Ravens Road

The plans for the extension to this property have now been passed; you can have sight/site of them at our offices at any time, and of course we will let you have copies of them as soon as possible.

The extension will have to incorporate many special features. I understand it is to house Mrs Fraser's Mother, who is elderly and whose eyesight/site is rapidly deteriorating.

I should like to meet you on sight/site early next week to go through the building details with you. Would you ring to make an appointment, please?

Yours sincerely

F Baker
ARCHITECT

Check your work, please. In the first two paragraphs the word should be 'sight'; in each case it is to do with seeing something. In the third paragraph it should be 'site', because Mr Baker is talking about the place where they are to meet.

Practice

The following is an extract from an article in a local newspaper about where to build the new leisure centre. Write or key it.

- Where you see - - - - - - - - choose one of the words or phrases from the list below.
- Where you see something like [   ] use quotation marks.
- For *direct quotations* of what people said, use double quotation marks.
- For *words* which need to be highlighted because they are unusual, or because it would make the article easier to read, use single quotation marks.

List of words or phrases to use
a lot of/alot of; sight/site; onaccount of/on account of; in fact/infact; all right/ alright/allright.

At the Council's meeting last Thursday it was agreed that the question of a convenient - - - - - - - - - - for the new leisure complex would be the subject of a public enquiry. Council leader Robert Dark thought the matter too important to be decided at this stage. [People must have the opportunity to make their views known,] he said.

Many councillors were opposed to this delay because - - - - - - - - - - - time had already been spent on the plans.

Members of the High Street Preservation Society are bitterly opposed to the proposed - - - - - - - - - - , because it would mean changing the whole mediaeval character of the town centre. [As far as we're concerned, it's - - - - - - - - - - to put the new complex on the outskirts of the town, but not in the centre,] said Mrs Jean Goodman, spokeswoman for the Society.

The developers, Johnson & Knight, think the new complex will not be an eyesore, as some people have said, but a very pleasant place for - - - - - - - - seers to gather. - - - - - - - - - - they are sure it will make the town more attractive to visitors.

The enquiry is unlikely to get underway until the New Year - - - - - - - - - - - the number of people who want to attend.

Points to remember from this chapter

Quotation marks (inverted commas)
- When writing dialogue, use double quotation marks
    - Put anything actually said in quotation marks
    - Always start the sentence that is said with a capital letter
    - Finish the spoken sentence with a comma if it is followed by 'he said' etc, except when a question mark or an exclamation mark is needed
    - Finish the spoken sentence with a full stop or its equivalent if nothing follows
    - In spoken sentences broken by 'he said' etc, end the first half with a comma and start the second half with a small letter
    - Start a new line for each person who speaks
- For actual quotations from what other people have written or said, use single or double quotation marks
- Use single quotation marks to highlight words or phrases if:
    - they are unusual
    - it would make the sentence easier to read

Common phrases
Do not run words together when they should be separate – check with the list.

Sight/site
Sight is to do with seeing
Site is to do with place - this is IT.

10 Semi-colons and Colons

Learning goals:
- When and how to use a semi-colon
- When and how to use a colon
- To lie and to lay
- Different from/to/than

■ When and how to use a semi-colon

A semi-colon is half way between a full stop and a comma (;), and that is one of its uses – a punctuation mark which is less definite than a full stop, but carries more weight than a comma.

It has two main uses:

- To break up a long sentence where the idea is the same. A full stop in the middle would be wrong, but the sentence is too long if it has only a comma in the middle of it.
- To break up the items in a list. These can be in a sentence or indented (set in from the margin) and displayed like a small table or chart.

A semi-colon which is used to break up a sentence

If your sentence is too long, but you do not want to break the train of thought with a full stop, try using a semi-colon.

Read this sentence aloud:

He was trying to park the car by reversing into a space, but could not get it at the right angle; he kept hitting the kerb with the rear wheels and having to start all over again.

The whole idea is the same, but the sentence would be rather long if it did not have a break. A full stop in the middle would be a little too emphatic.

Notice that each half of the sentence – before and after the semi-colon – is itself a sentence with a subject and a verb. 'He' is the subject in both halves; the verb in the first half is 'was trying' and in the second half is 'kept hitting'. Many people make the mistake of leaving the subject and/or the verb, or part of the verb, out of the second half of the sentence. They might write 'He was trying to park the car by reversing into a space, but could not get it at the right angle; hitting the kerb with the rear wheels and having to start all over again.' Strictly speaking, this is wrong, but is done so frequently it is almost acceptable.

Here are two rules to follow when using a semi-colon to break up a long sentence:

USE A SEMI-COLON WHEN YOU WANT A PUNCTUATION MARK WHICH IS LIGHTER THAN A FULL STOP BUT HEAVIER THAN A COMMA

EACH HALF OF THE SENTENCE – BEFORE AND AFTER THE SEMI-COLON – SHOULD ITSELF BE A SENTENCE, WITH A SUBJECT AND A VERB

A semi-colon used in a list

Semi-colons are very useful to separate items in a list, particularly when the items are more than one word long. Read aloud this sentence:

The following are included: interpersonal skills, listening skills, body language and personal space and opening and closing a conversation.

Here commas have been used, quite correctly, with commas between the items in the list, but 'and' between the last two (see Chapter 2). However, it is difficult to decide which are the last two, and which items go together. If you write the list with semi-colons instead, it is easier to read:

The following are included: interpersonal skills; listening skills; body language and personal space; opening and closing a conversation.

Notice that you do not need 'and' to join the final two items.

Semi-colons can also be used in an indented list. For example:

Press ENTER to:
        confirm a command;
        jump to the next infill space;
        call up the next menu.

In this example the sentence is written in the same way as if it had been written along the line. Sometimes people start each indented line with a capital letter, like this:

Press ENTER to:
>Confirm a command;
>Jump to the next infill space;
>Call up the next menu.

It does not matter which you do, as long as you are consistent.

Exercise on using semi-colons to break up long sentences and in lists

This is part of a letter you have received from your Building Society. Write or key it. Whenever you come to a comma, decide whether it would be better to use a semi-colon. (Normally one space is left after a semi-colon.)

Dear (your own name)

Thank you for reporting the loss of your cash card, your promptness in doing so has meant that we have been able to register its loss immediately.

You should now

>Confirm the loss in writing,
>Complete the enclosed form,
>Inform us if the card is found.

It was fairly obvious that semi-colons would be useful after 'cash card', 'writing' and 'form'. As you can see, they are not difficult to use and can be very helpful to the reader.

■ When and how to use a colon

Like semi-colons, colons are used in two ways. They are used to introduce a list, as they have been frequently throughout this book, and are often preceded by the phase 'as follows'. They can also be used in the middle of a sentence when the second half of the sentence expands on or explains the first.

A colon used to introduce a list

As you know, this is a very common use of a colon (:). Some people write it with a dash after it (:-); this is quite acceptable, but does not add anything of value.
The list following the colon can be:

within a sentence;
in the form of lettered or numbered paragraphs;
indented, fairly short items.

As you see from this example, and from those used earlier in this chapter, it is often used to introduce lists which are divided by semi-colons.
One mistake which many people make is not so much the use of the colon itself, but in the way they write words before and the list which follows the colon. For example, read this sentence aloud:

Before turning off the power please ensure that:

Your own screen is back on the main menu;
Check that everyone else has exited from the program;
All documents are saved.

You should read each part of the sentence separately, to see if it makes sense. 'Please ensure that - your own screen is back on the main menu,' makes sense. 'Please ensure that - all documents are saved.' also makes sense. 'Please ensure that - check that everyone else has exited from the program,' does not make sense.
The sentence can be improved in one of two ways.
Either alter the words *before* the colon to read:

Before turning off the power, please:
(and *after* the colon)

Make sure that your own screen is back on the main menu;
Check that everyone else has exited from the program;
Make sure that all documents are saved.

Or

leave the words *before* the colon as they are and alter the second item in the list, so that it reads:

Before turning off the power, please make sure that:

Everyone else has exited from the program;

You must make sure that the items in the list match, and make sense if they are read separately. Sometimes it is better to alter the words before the colon and sometimes it is better to alter the beginning of the item in the list. Sometimes you have to do both.

USE A COLON(:) TO INTRODUCE A LIST

MAKE SURE EACH SEPARATE PART OF THE SENTENCE
MAKES SENSE

A colon used in the middle of a sentence

A colon is used much less often in this way, but it can be a very helpful punctuation mark, and just the thing to make the sentence easier to read and clearer in meaning.
It divides a sentence into two, where the second half expands on or explains the first half. For example, in the sentence:

'Pressing RETURN will take you down to the next line: it is like doing a carriage return on a typewriter.'

the first half, before the colon, tells you what pressing RETURN actually does; the second half of the sentence gives an illustration which would be particularly helpful to typists. The second half is expanding on the first.

'The bottle was nearly empty: most of the wine had been drunk.'

is another example of the second half of the sentence explaining the first. It is often the case of saying the same thing in a slightly different way to make it clearer.

USE A COLON IN THE MIDDLE OF A SENTENCE
WHEN YOU WANT TO ILLUSTRATE, EXPLAIN OR EXPAND
ON WHAT YOU HAVE JUST SAID

Exercise in using colons to introduce a list and in the middle of a sentence

This is the next paragraph of the letter from your Building Society. Write or key it. Use colons and semi-colons whenever you think it is right to do so. If you are keying, leave one space after a colon and a semi-colon.

If you find your card, please let us know where and when you found it this helps us to identify any misuse of the card in the meantime. Please specify exactly where it was found the date and time at which it was found where you think it had been between the time of your losing it and finding it again.

Your completed paragraph could look like this:

If you find your card, please let us know where and when you found it: this helps us to identify any misuse of the card in the meantime. Please specify: exactly where it was found; the date and time at which it was found; where you think it had been between the time of your losing it and finding it again.

■ To lie and to lay

These are very confusing verbs. This is what they mean:

to lie = to tell a lie
to lie = to lie down
to lay = to put something or someone down (to lay a carpet, or an egg)
It is something you do to something else, not yourself

The confusion happens because many parts of the three verbs are spelt in the same way. Study these tables:

To lie (tell a lie)

PRESENT		PAST	
I lie	we lie	I lied	we lied
you lie	you lie	you lied	you lied
he/she/it lies	they lie	he/she/it lied	they lied
or			
		I have lied	we have lied
		you have lied	you have lied
		he/she/it has lied	they have lied
I am lying when I say . . .		I was lying when I said . . .	

To lie (lie down)

PRESENT		*PAST*	
I lie	we lie	I lay	we lay
you lie	you lie	you lay	you lay
he/she/it lies	they lie	he/she/it lay	they lay
		or	
		I have lain	we have lain
		you have lain	you have lain
		he/she/it has lain	they have lain
I am lying on the floor		I was *lying* on the floor	

To lay (put something down)

PRESENT		*PAST*	
I lay	we lay	I laid	we laid
you lay	you lay	you laid	you laid
he/she/it lays	they lay	he/she/it laid	they laid
		or	
		I have laid	we have laid
		you have laid	you have laid
		he/she/it has laid	they have laid
I am laying the carpet		She was laying an egg	

You can see from the table that to say 'I was laying on the bed' is wrong. 'Lay down!' when you are telling someone to lie down is also wrong. You can lay down wine in a cellar, but not yourself!

Another phrase which people get wrong is about lying in bed in the morning. You should have a lie-in, not a lay-in.

Use the tables as a reference when you do the next exercise.

Exercise on to lie and to lay

The next paragraph of the letter from the Building Society tells you what you should do to avoid losing the new card, when you get it. Write or key this; when you see L _____, use the right part of the verb.

When you receive your new card, please do not leave it L_____ around for someone else to pick up. When you are getting money out of the cash dispenser, do not L_____the card on the ledge: keep it in your hand. We are not suggesting that you were L_____ when you said you thought it had been stolen, but it is a fact that personal carelessness is usually the cause of lost cards. We have known instances where a card has L _____ in the gutter for a long time before someone has picked it up and returned it to us.

What would you think of a lecture like that from a Building Society? They would probably write something a lot less dictatorial, but what is written in that paragraph would be the underlying message. Check your work with the correct version which you will find in the Practice section of this chapter.

■ Different from/to/than

The correct version is 'different *from*', because if a thing is different, it is not the same as another thing: it is going away *from* it.
    'Different to' is technically wrong, but is used by very many people, and so has become accepted. You would not be penalised for using it, but you might offend some people.
    'Different than' is American.

DIFFERENT FROM IS RIGHT
DIFFERENT TO IS ACCEPTABLE
DIFFERENT THAN IS AMERICAN

Practice

Write a reply to your Building Society telling them that you have found your cash card in the pocket of your jeans. It has been through the washing machine and is now unusable – please may you have another one. Apologise for the trouble you have caused, and return the card with your letter. Assure them that you will take better care of the card next time. Make sure the style of your letter is appropriate. You really could do with another card, so be formal and polite, but do not grovel. This does not mean that you have to use long words: keep the words, and the sentences, short. Do not use conversational words like 'great' or 'OK'.
    In writing your letter you must use:

- At least one semi-colon
- At least one colon
- At least one part of to lie, to lie or to lay; if you can include one part of all three verbs, so much the better
- The expression 'different from' at least once.

This is the full text of the letter from the Building Society, to which your letter is the reply.

Dear (your own name)

Thank you for reporting the loss of your cash card; your promptness in doing so has meant that we have been able to register its loss immediately.

You should now

Confirm the loss in writing;
Complete the enclosed form;
Inform us if the card is found.

If you find your card, please let us know where and when you found it: this helps us to identify any misuse of the card in the meantime. Please specify: exactly where it was found; the date and time at which it was found; where you think it had been between the time of your losing it and finding it again.

When you receive your new card, please do not leave it lying around for someone else to pick up. When you are getting money out of the cash dispenser, do not lay the card on the ledge: keep it in your hand. We are not suggesting that you were lying when you said you thought it had been stolen, but it is a fact that personal carelessness is usually the cause of lost cards. We have known instances where a card has lain in the gutter for a long time before someone has picked it up and returned it to us.

We look forward to hearing from you.

Yours sincerely

(Mrs) A JARRETT
Assistant Manager

Enclosure

Points to remember from this chapter

Semi-colons

- A semi-colon is lighter than a full stop but heavier than a comma
- Use a semi-colon (;) to break up a long sentence
- Each part of the broken sentence should be a sentence in itself
- Use a semi-colon to separate the items in a list

Colons

- Use a colon (:) (no dash needed) to introduce a list
- Make sure the items in the list match – each part must make sense
- Use a colon in the middle of a sentence when you want to illustrate, explain or expand on what you have just said

To lie (tell a lie); to lie (lie down); to lay (put something somewhere)

✓ RIGHT	X WRONG
It was left lying about	It was left laying about
He laid down the law	He lay down the law
Lie on the floor, please	Lay on the floor, please
Lay the clothes on the bed, please	Lie the clothes on the bed, please

Different

- Different 'from' (away from) is right
- Different 'to' is acceptable
- Different 'than' is American

11 Hyphens, Dashes and Brackets

Learning goals:
- When and how to use hyphens
- When and how to use dashes
- When and how to use brackets
- Brackets and full stops
- None
- Stationary/stationery

Hyphens (-) are symbols used to join words or parts of words. Dashes (–) and brackets ([]) are used to separate one part of a sentence from another.

■ When and how to use hyphens

Hyphens have three main uses:

1 To join two or more words to make one, often an adjective,
   eg 'gold-rimmed'.
2 To join a prefix to a word, eg ante-natal, anti-smoking. A prefix is
   something which is stuck on, or fixed, to the beginning of a word.
3 To split a word at the end of a line.

HYPHENS DO NOT HAVE SPACES BEFORE AND AFTER THEM

Hyphens used to join two or more words

A hyphen makes sure that the reader reads the word as one word, not two.
For example:

'Gold is a yellow-coloured metal.' (It is yellow-coloured.)

is different from:

'Gold is a yellow, coloured metal.' (It is yellow and coloured.)

If you are in doubt about whether to use a hyphen in this way, ask yourself
'Are the words I want to use really one word?'

An up-to-date diary; a free-for-all; blue-green algae; one-tenth;
long-lasting; pigeon-toed;

These are all examples of words joined together to make one; as you can see,
many of them are adjectives.

Note: Hyphens are much less frequently used than they used to be.

Exercise using hyphens to join two or more words

Write or key these sentences. Insert hyphens where they are needed. Do not
leave a space before or after a hyphen.

1   The two toned filing cabinet matches the rest of the office furniture.
2   Housekeeping the disks includes a clear out of redundant files.
3   Visit our stand for a really down to earth approach to your photocopying
    needs.
4   Every office should have an easy to use fax machine.
5   Workstations are purpose built.

You should have hyphenated, in alphabetical order, clear-out; down-to-earth;
easy-to-use; purpose-built; two-toned.

Hyphens used to join a prefix to a word

Examples of prefixes are anti-, ante-, co-, de-, re-. They are used in words like:

anti-freeze; co-operate; de-icer; re-appraisal; ante-post (betting); co-respondent; de-contamination; re-record.

The hyphen joins the prefix to the word, and yet separates the prefix from the word, so that the whole word is easy to read, particularly when the main word starts with a vowel, like 'de-icer'. 'Deicer' would be very difficult to read properly without the hyphen to help!

Exercise using hyphens to join a prefix to a word

Write or key these sentences. Insert hyphens where they are needed. Do not leave a space before or after a hyphen.

6   On this phone you can leave prerecorded messages.
7   An antistatic mat can prevent small electric shocks when you are using the printer.
8   Please rerecord the message on the answering machine.
9   Please do not switch the computer off overnight; your cooperation would be much appreciated.
10 The Managing Director and his Codirectors will have to take the final decision on the new system.

Check your work. The following should have been hyphenated: pre-recorded, anti-static, re-record, co-operation (some people do not hyphenate this word), Co-directors.

Hyphens used to split a word at the end of a line

When you are keying, you do not normally have to think about where to split a word at the end of a line to avoid ragged line endings; the wraparound facility takes the whole word to the next line for you.

However, you do sometimes need to know when to split a word, These are the usual rules:

- Do not split words of only one syllable eg 'thought'.
- Do not split names eg 'Mar-garet', 'Jona-than'.
- Split words at natural breaks if possible, for example if a word is made up of two words eg 'wrap-around'.

- Try to keep the basic word as a word.
  - put the beginning of the word on one line and the basic word on the next eg inter-national (the beginning of a word is often a prefix).
  - put the basic word on one line and the ending on the next eg accommodation.
- The first letter on the next line should be a consonant if possible.
- You can split a word between double consonants eg accom-modate.

There are other rules which some people use, but if you follow the ones mentioned here, you could not be penalised. If you are in doubt about a short word, it is better to put the whole thing on the next line.

Exercise using hyphens to split a word at the end of a line

Refer to the rules written above, and write or key these sentences. Split the last word at the end of the first line in each sentence. Do *not* leave a space at the beginning of the next line.

11 Electricians will be checking the wiring circuits throughout
   the day.
12 I have left the draft with all its amendments
   in the 'Out' tray.
13 Ceefax and Oracle are the television networks' databases
   called teletext.
14 The teletext services are not interactive
   – you can only read what is there.
15 The warning light has been repaired; the decontamination
   area has still to be checked.

Check your work. It would be sensible to split these words as follows: through-out; amend-ments; data-bases; inter-active; de-contamination or de-contamina-tion, depending on how much room you had left on the line.

A HYPHEN CAN JOIN WORDS TO MAKE ONE
OR SPLIT THEM FOR EASE OF READING

NO SPACES BEFORE AND AFTER

■ When and how to use dashes

A dash is the same symbol as a hyphen (–), but a dash has a space before and a space after it. Although it is the same symbol, it is a completely different form of punctuation.

Dashes in pairs

Dashes normally, although not always, go in pairs, and are rather like brackets. They separate a phrase in the middle of the sentence from the rest of the sentence; they are used to highlight or explain what has just gone before.

For example, in the sentence:

Graphics can really liven up a presentation – in black and white or colour – so that it makes a real impact.

the phrase ' – in black and white or colour – ' adds information, or illustrates what has gone before, but the sentence would make perfectly good sense without it. In some ways dashes are like a pair of commas (see Chapter 2), but add more weight to the punctuation, because they stand out more.

A pair of dashes is never used at the end of a sentence – always in the middle.

Exercise using dashes in pairs

Write or key these sentences, inserting a pair of dashes in each.

16 Switch the terminal off using the rocker switch at the back and on again.
17 Select the option copy, move or delete from the menu.
18 Check carefully before you give the final command ie press ENTER to erase the file.
19 When you see the message SYNTAX ERROR syntax in this context means construction it means you have keyed something in incorrectly.
20 Make back-up copies sometimes referred to as security copies of all important files.

-   In sentence 16 'using the rocker switch at the back' explains how you switch off and on again; it could take a pair of dashes.
-   In sentence 17 the options 'copy, move or delete' are listed, and could go within dashes.

- Sentence 18 is similar to sentence 16: 'ie press ENTER' tells you how to do what you are asked to do.
- In sentence 19 'syntax in this context means construction' is an explanation of what SYNTAX is.
- In sentence 20 'sometimes referred to as security copies' expands on the phrase 'back-up' copies.

You have used dashes to EXPLAIN, ILLUSTRATE and EXPAND UPON a phrase in the middle of a sentence, just as if you had used a colon. However:

- you cannot use a colon in the middle of a sentence.
- you could just as easily have used brackets, which you will be studying shortly.

A single dash

There are two instances when you can use a single dash as a punctuation mark:

1 Instead of a colon;
2 As an indicator for indented, listed items.

It is also used, of course, as a symbol for minus ($4 - 2 = 2$), and as a symbol for 'to' eg Glasgow–Edinburgh; 0800-0900. When it means 'minus' or 'to', you can leave a space either side of the dash or not, as you choose. Be consistent!

A dash instead of a colon

A single dash towards the end of a sentence can be used instead of colon. In the sentence earlier in this chapter: 'A pair of dashes is never used at the end of a sentence – always in the middle.' it is used very much in this way. Use it when you need to add a little something which will not, in itself, be a complete sentence.

It is used in headings in a similar way – eg:

INFORMATION TECHNOLOGY – THE STATE OF THE ART

A dash as an indicator for indented, listed items

In this case dashes are used instead of numbers or letters to separate one short paragraph or item from another. They were used in this way earlier in this chapter:

- In sentence 16 . . .
- In sentence 17 . . . etc.

There is no exercise for this section on using a single dash, but you can refer to it if you need to.

■ When and how to use brackets

Brackets in a sentence *always* go in pairs. They can be round (), square [] or sometimes curly {}. They are used in very much the same way as dashes. They explain, illustrate or expand upon what has gone before; without the phrase in brackets, the sentence still makes sense.

Exercise using brackets

Write or key these sentences, inserting a pair of brackets in each. Leave a space before the opening bracket, no space after it, no space before the closing bracket, one space after it.

21 The QWERTY keyboard Q-W-E-R-T-Y are the six letters on the top, left of the keyboard is the most commonly used.

22 Desk Top Publishing DTP can improve the image of the dullest document.

23 The Health and Safety at Work Act usually referred to as HASAWA covers responsibilities for safe working practices of employers and employees.

24 Make sure your adjustable chair the type with the back rest is at the right height.

25 Pre-printed forms eg Order Forms are very difficult to do on a computer, unless they are specifically designed for that system.

The bracketed phrases should have been: eg Order Forms; the type with the back rest; usually referred to as HASAWA; DTP; Q-W-E-R-T-Y are the six letters on the top, left of the keyboard. As you can see, you could equally well have used a pair of dashes instead. Check your spacing, for example sentence 22 should be: Desk Top Publishing (DTP) can improve the image of the dullest document.

BRACKETS IN A SENTENCE ARE ALWAYS IN PAIRS

■ Brackets and full stops

Should the full stop come inside the closing bracket or outside it? It depends. This is the rule:

1   If the *whole sentence* is inside brackets the full stop must be *inside* the closing bracket.
2   If a *bracketed phrase* finishes a sentence, the full stop must come *outside* the closing bracket.

For example:

A   When naming your documents, give them a name which has some meaning. (Please refer to the chapter on document management.)
B   When naming your documents, give them a name which has some meaning (eg CONTRACT).

In example 'A', '(Please refer to the chapter on document management.)' is a whole sentence inside brackets. The full stop goes *inside* the closing bracket. In example 'B', '(eg CONTRACT)' is the final phrase in the sentence. The full stop goes *outside* the closing bracket.

Exercise on brackets and full stops

Here are five more sentences to write or key. All you have to do this time is to insert the full stop, or its equivalent, in the right place.

26   The information is collected from each terminal overnight (between midnight and 0600 hours)
27   The printout of sales statistics is sent to each outlet weekly. (To send them daily would not be cost-effective)
28   The sales last week exceeded £90,000 (is this a record?)
29   The sales in the previous week were only £40,000. (Is this an all-time low)
30   The van driver arrives with the goods and the disk. (The disk is checked against the goods actually delivered (not necessarily ordered))

Check your work with these correct versions:

26 The information is collected from each terminal overnight (between midnight and 0600 hours).
27 The printout of sales statistics is sent to each outlet weekly. (To send them daily would not be cost-effective.)
28 The sales last week exceeded £90,000 (is this a record?).
29 The sales in the previous week were only £40,000. (Is this an all-time low?)
30 The van driver arrives with the goods and the disk. (The disk is checked against the goods actually delivered (not necessarily ordered).)

Sentence 30 looks a little odd, but is quite correct. The full stop must be inside the closing bracket, because you are dealing with a complete sentence, but outside the closing bracket of the phrase '(not necessarily ordered)'. To avoid peculiar-looking punctuation like this, you could have used a single dash instead of the second pair of brackets: (The disk is checked against the goods actually delivered – not necessarily ordered.)

WHOLE SENTENCE = FULL STOP INSIDE CLOSING BRACKET

FINAL PHRASE = FULL STOP OUTSIDE CLOSING BRACKET

■ None

None can mean one of two things:

- not any, (not one) or
- no-one or not one

None meaning 'not any'

If none means 'not any' then 'he has not got none' must be wrong, because you are saying 'he has not got not any', which is nonsense.

In conversation you are unlikely to say 'He has not got none.' You are much more likely to say 'He hasn't got none.' or 'He ain't got none.' These are all wrong. You should say, or write, 'He hasn't got any.' 'He has not got any.' In the same way 'He hasn't got no idea.' is also wrong. It should be 'He hasn't got any idea.' or 'He has no idea.'

None meaning no-one or not one

The point about none meaning 'not one' or 'no-one' is that it takes singular verb. So in a sentence like:

'None of the terminals is up and running.'

the verb is singular – none *is*. (See Chapter 5)

You will often see people write, or hear them say 'None of the terminals (or whatever) are . . .'. This is technically wrong, but is used by so many people it is acceptable.

Exercise using none

Here are three sentences to write or key. Where you see a gap or an alternative, use the correct word.

    31 None of the operators has/have totally mastered the software.
    32 They did not have _____ training.
    33 When asked what instruction they had had, they answered that they had not had _____.

NONE MEANING NO-ONE OR NOT ONE TAKES A *SINGULAR* VERB
HE HASN'T GOT NONE IS *WRONG*
HE HAS NOT GOT NO IDEA IS *WRONG*

■ Stationary/stationery

Here is a way of remembering which is which:

Stationary (with an 'a') stands still
Stationery (with an 'e') includes envelopes

Exercise on stationary/stationery

Write or key these two final sentences on the office and information technology theme. When you see stationary/stationery, choose the correct word.

34 Continuous stationary/stationery usually needs a feeder attached to the printer to keep it straight.

35 A company which is not progressive in its information technology policy will not only remain stationary/stationery in this competitive market, but will probably go backwards.

Practice

This chapter ends its information technology theme with a summary of three paragraphs about Desk Top Publishing.

Summarise these paragraphs in not more than 80 words.

Make a copy by writing or keying it, making sure that the layout and presentation are good.

In your summary, which you should entitle DESK TOP PUBLISHING, you must use the following words and phrases, correctly punctuated:

'(usually the most popular feature)'
'– which sometimes clash'
'well-researched decision'.

Desk Top Publishing (DTP) is not a glorified method of producing word-processing printouts. It is much more than that. Advertisements can lead potential users to believe that they can produce exquisite printouts, made into booklets or leaflets, at the press of a button or two, but this is not so.

The actual capacity to produce exactly what the user wants depends, as ever, on the hardware needed to produce the final output, and the software required to facilitate the input. As with every other item of information technology, the user must know, and know in detail, exactly what is essential and what is desirable in a DTP system. Obviously the hardware must include a keyboard, screen and laser printer, but is a scanner a necessary part of the configuration? Will the software be required to include a graphics capability (this is normally the DTP feature which most people think they need) or will good text manipulation facilities be sufficient?

The skills required to use a full DTP system are considerable. Operators will need not only logical minds and patience to manipulate the text and incorporate the graphics, but also a certain flair for design and layout. They will also have to learn a whole new vocabulary, which could include printers' terms as well as information technology terms – and these sometimes clash. They must accept the fact that they will not master these skills overnight.

Points to remember from this chapter

- HYPHENS make two or more words into one.
  They join a prefix to a word.
  They are used to split a word at the end of a line.
  They do not take a space either side of them.
- DASHES and BRACKETS in the middle of a sentence are used in pairs.
  Dashes need a space either side of them.
- A FULL STOP comes *inside* the closing bracket if the bracketed words are a *whole sentence.*
  A FULL STOP comes *outside* the closing bracket if the bracketed words are the *final phrase* in a sentence.
- They haven't got no . . . . is *wrong.*
- They haven't got any . . . . is *right.*
- NONE of these *is.*
- STATIONARY stands still.
- STATIONERY includes envelopes.

12 Abbreviations

Learning goals:
- The common abbreviations eg, etc, ie. NB, pp, PS
- Time, weight and measurement abbreviations
- Whose/who's/who/whom
- Teach/learn
- Them/those

■ The common abbreviations eg, etc, ie, NB, pp, PS

These abbreviations are frequently used in formal business English, but are often incorrectly spelled or used in the wrong way. For each abbreviation here is a table showing what it is short for, what it means and an example of its use. The examples are taken from a procedure manual for the checkouts in a DIY store.

ABBREVIATIONS DO NOT NEED FULL STOPS
(See Chapter 2)

Abbreviation	Short for	Meaning	Example
eg	*exempli gratia*	for example	For bulky items (eg wheelbarrows) . . .
etc (*not* ect)	*et cetera*	and the rest	Small items – nails, screws, tacks etc . .
ie	*id est*	that is	When signing on – ie when you key in your password . . .

NB	*Nota bene*	note well, please note	NB Remember to put the credit card voucher in the till drawer
pp	*per pro*	for and on behalf of	Sign this on behalf of the Checkout Supervisor - sign your own name and write pp next to the Supervisor's name
PS	*Post scriptum*	after the main text (usually in a letter)	Dear Customer. . Yours sincerely . . PS Please pass this Promotion Voucher to a friend if you do not want to use it yourself

The mistakes people tend to make with these abbreviations are:

- Using eg when they mean ie and vice versa.
  Ask yourself whether you are giving an example; if you are, it must be eg. If not, it is probably ie.
- Writing ect instead of etc.
- Signing somebody else's name, which you should never do. Sign your own name on behalf of someone else, and use the abbreviation pp to make it clear that this is what you have done.

Exercise on using these common abbreviations

As you write or key these instructions taken from the DIY Checkout Manual, insert the correct abbreviation where there is a '?'.

ENTERING THE PRICES

1   Price tickets with their Price Look Up (PLU) codes are affixed to merchandise in specific places to make them easy to find quickly.

2   Price tickets for small items, particularly those in bubble packs (adhesives, nails, screws, washers '?'), are affixed to the top of the packet on the reverse.

3   Price tickets for bulky items ('?' bathroom cabinets, curtain poles, shower trays) are affixed on the end of the packaging, not on the sides.

4   Items which have been cut to size ('?' to a customer's particular requirements) will have the price written on them by the Sales Assistant. Key in the price, not the code.

5   If you over-ring an item, you must enter it on the Over-ring Pad and get it signed by the Checkout Supervisor or the Deputy '?' the Supervisor.

6   If you think the price which comes up on the screen is unrealistic for the merchandise concerned, CALL THE CHECKOUT SUPERVISOR immediately. It could be that a customer has switched tickets. '?' your vigilance could prevent theft.

Check your work. Reading these comments will help you:

- In sentence 6 you should have used NB – the Company wants Checkout Operators to be very well aware that prevention of theft is largely a matter of staff vigilance.
- In sentence 5 you should have used pp, because the Deputy signs for and on behalf of the Supervisor. (pp is also the abbreviation for 'pages' by the way.)
- In sentence 4 you should have used ie 'to a customer's particular requirements' explains what 'cut to size' is. It is another way of saying the same thing.
- In sentence 3 you should have used eg because you were giving examples of bulky items.
- In sentence 2 you should have used etc, spelled correctly. Etc always comes at the end of a phrase, whereas eg and ie come at the beginning.
- Sentence 1 had no abbreviations.

---

etc – not ect
eg   = for example
ie   = that is

■ Time, weight and measurement abbreviations

This table shows the abbreviations (metric where appropriate) you are most likely to use.

ABBREVIATIONS DO NOT NEED FULL STOPS

	Meaning	*Abbreviation*	*Origins*
TIME	hours	hrs	*ante meridian*
	in the morning	am	
	in the afternoon	pm	*post meridian*
	Before Christ	BC	
	In the year of our Lord	AD	*anno domini*
LENGTH	millimetre	mm	
	centimetre	cm	
	metre	m	
	kilometre	km	
	miles per hour	mph	
AREA	square centimetre	cm^2	
	square metre	m^2	
	hectare	ha	
	square kilometre	km^2	
VOLUME	cubic centimetre	cm^3	
	cubic metre	m^3	
	millilitre	ml	
	centilitre	cl	
	litre	l	
	miles per gallon	mpg	
WEIGHT	gram	g	
	kilogram	kg	
	tonne	t	

NB One ton is not the same as one tonne although they both have the same abbreviation (t). One ton is 20 cwt (hundredweight) in Imperial measure. One tonne is 1,000 kg. 1 ton = 1.0161 tonnes, which is not the same weight at all. If in doubt about which to use, check.

Should you have a space before using these abbreviations? It does not matter, provided you are consistent.

✓	X
RIGHT	WRONG
9.00 am – 10.00 am	9.00 am – 10.00am
9.00 am – 10.00 am	
0900 hrs – 1000 hrs	0900hrs – 10.00 hrs

You will notice that the time in the 24-hour clock is written here without a full stop. This is the normal way of writing it, but you will sometimes see it written with a full stop (eg 09.00 hrs). It does not matter, provided you are consistent.

Exercise on time, weight and measurement abbreviations

This is another extract from the DIY Checkout Procedure Manual. Whenever you see a measurement of any sort in brackets - eg (2 metres), put in the abbreviation instead (2 m).

HANDLING THE CUSTOMER'S PURCHASES

1   Take care of customers' purchases. The sale is not complete until the merchandise arrives home in good condition.
2   Do not put a (2 litre) can of paint on top of a packet of light bulbs.
3   Make sure that wood more than (1 metre) long does not fall off the end of the checkout.
4   Check that bags of ready-mixed cement – particularly the smaller, (5 kilogram) size – are not split and liable to spil!.
5   Although the store closes officially at (2100 hours), do not rush through an order which comes to your checkout at (2058 hours).

Your abbreviations should have been 2 1; 1 m; 5 kg; 2100 hrs; 2058 hrs.

■ Whose/who's/who/whom

Whose and who's

Whose and who's is like its and it's.

- WHOSE is *possessive* (belonging to someone)
- WHO'S is short for *who is*

For example, in the sentence:

'The operator whose till is the most accurate will get a bonus.'

the till belongs to the operator. It is like using her, his, our, your etc.
In the sentence:

'The operator who's using the end till usually gets more business.'

who's is short for who is.

As we said in Chapter 8, you should not normally use omission apostrophes in formal written English. Therefore you should not need to use 'who's' at all, except in dialogue or in very informal communications.

Who and whom

WHO is like 'he', 'she' or 'they'
WHOM is like 'him', 'her' or 'them'

The easiest way to remember whether you should use 'who' or 'whom' is to substitute, in your mind, 'he/him', 'she/her' or 'they/them'.
So, when you see a sentence like:

'The customer, to who/whom I had given the receipt, brought the goods back the next day.'

say to yourself: 'If the sentence were round the other way, I would have given the receipt to him (or her), not to he (or she).' So it must be 'whom'.

Try this sentence:

'The Managers, who/whom the Directors had met at the Conference, all thought the idea a good one.'

Ask yourself, 'Did the Directors meet 'them' or 'they'?' The answer, of course, is 'them', so you should use 'whom'.

Now try this one:

'The cook, who/whom was a cheerful sort of person, always started work at 8.00 am.'

Here you could easily substitute she (not her) for who/whom, so the answer must be to use 'who'. This is not a sentence you would normally get wrong. You are much more likely to write or say 'who' when it should be 'whom'; although many people no longer use 'whom' at all.

Exercise on whose/who's/who/whom

The Checkout Manual continues with instructions on what to do with a Credit Card. Write or key these instructions. Where you see w- - - - -, use the correct word: whose, who's, who or whom.

CREDIT CARDS
1 When a customer presents you with a Credit Card, run the card through the card reader to check its authenticity.
2 Ring up the customer's purchases.
3 Ask the customer w- - - - has presented the card to sign the till slip, which doubles as a Credit Card Voucher.
4 Check that the person w- - - - signature is on the back of the card is likely to be the customer with w- - - - you are dealing - eg is a woman using a card with a man's name on it?
5 Give the card and one copy of the Credit Card Voucher to the customer, w- - - - is waiting for it.
6 NB Remember to put the other copy of the Credit Card Voucher in the till drawer.

Check whether your work is correct:

- In sentence 3 the word should be 'who'. Would you be able to substitute he/ she or him/her? The answer must be that he/she has presented the card, so you should have used 'who'.
- In sentence 4 the signature belongs to the customer, so you should have used 'whose'.
- In the same sentence, were you dealing with he/she or him/her? The answer is him/her, so you should have used 'whom'.
- In sentence 5 he or she is waiting for the card, so you should have used 'who'. You should not have been tempted to abbreviate 'who is' to 'who's'.

■ Teach/learn

Teach something to someone
Learn something from someone

This pair of words is like lend/borrow (see Chapter 5). You have to ask yourself which way the teaching or learning is going. Another way of remembering is to say that teachers teach and learners learn.

To say 'Will you learn me how to drive?' is wrong.
It should be 'Will you teach me how to drive?'

■ Them/those

'Them' cannot be used as if it were the word 'those'.

To say 'Pass me them scissors.' is *wrong*. You must say 'Pass me those scissors.'
'Pass them to me' is of course, quite correct. 'Them' always stands on its own – do not try to use it with a noun.

Exercise on teach/learn and them/those

The final extract from the DIY Checkout Manual uses teach, learn, them and those. Write or key these instructions on training procedures. When you see TEACH/LEARN or THEM/THOSE, choose the correct word.

INSTRUCTIONS TO CHECKOUT SUPERVISORS
1   Make sure that each Checkout Operator is properly trained. TEACH/ LEARN each operator all the necessary procedures in the training room.
2   Make sure that each Operator can TEACH/LEARN in the best circumstances. Training should be not interrupted.
3   TEACH/LEARN all Operators the skills of customer care. Customers are our lifeblood. TEACH/LEARN the Operators to treat THEM/THOSE as such.
4   Also make sure that THEM/THOSE Operators who work part-time receive all the training they need.

Check that you are right. You should have used the words in this sequence: teach; learn; teach; them; those.

Practice

Having worked on the instructions to Checkout Operators and Supervisors, write some instructions yourself; use one of these subjects:

- Wiring a 3-pin plug
- Travel instructions on how to reach your home from another point in your locality
- Applying eye makeup
- How to set a video recorder.

Writing instructions requires you to be very logical and precise. Please follow these instructions carefully:

1   Choose a subject you know you can do. A learner cannot learn from a teacher who does not know what he or she is talking about.
2   Get your points in a logical order before you start to write.
3   Give your instructions a precise heading.
4   Number your instructions.
5   Write each instruction clearly and concisely so that the learner can do what you say. It is often helpful to start each instruction with a verb.
6   Use each of the following somewhere in your instructions: eg; ie; etc; NB.
7   Use one or more of the time, weight, volume, length or area abbreviations if you can.

When you have finished, give your instructions to someone else to see whether they can be followed. If possible, get the other person to try out what you have written – under your supervision.

Points to remember from this chapter

- etc, not ect
  eg = for example
  ie = that is
- Abbreviations do not need full stops
- Be consistent about spacing
- Beware ton and tonne
- WHOSE is like its
- WHO'S is like it's
  WHO is like he, she or they
  WHOM is like him, her or them
- Teachers teach to
  Learners learn from
- 'Them things' is *wrong*
  'Those things' is *right*

13 Writing for Special Occasions

Learning goals: • Style, tone and format which suit the occasion

Throughout this book you have been reading and writing English in a variety of styles, tones and formats. Some examples are:

- A chatty promotional letter trying to sell luggage
- Formal Memos
- Instructions on operating a photocopier or a DIY checkout
- Messages from a hotel receptionist.

Good English language skills include the right tone, style and format for each piece of writing. Presentation is very important, too, whether your piece is handwritten or keyed.

This chapter gives you practice in several different sorts of writing. Work through the material in any order, checking your grammar, spelling and punctuation and following the instructions given.

Practice

Practice 1 – A letter of complaint

This is a letter about something you saw in an advert in the local paper. You ordered it but it has not arrived.

When writing a letter of complaint, remember what you probably want most is your complaint dealt with - you do not necessarily want a lot of hassle. The best way to go about this is to:

- express distress at what has happened
- set out the facts of the case and
- make definite proposals about what you want done next.

If you write really angry letters, you will not get the best service from the recipient.

Keep the tone formal and polite, but firm. This is what has happened:

As a result of seeing their letter in the weekend press, some four weeks ago you ordered a set of monogrammed towels from De Luxe Drapers Ltd of 68 London Lane Bolton Greater Manchester BL4 2DW. The set was a bargain, priced at £24.95 including VAT and carriage.

You are very annoyed that you have not yet received the set, which was ordered as a present for a relation whose birthday is now only ten days away.

No explanation has been received from the company, nor has it been possible to contact them by telephone as they are always engaged.

You know that the order has been received because a recent bank statement shows that your cheque was presented for payment within a few days of sending off the order.

Write a letter of complaint, following these instructions:

1   Write from your home address - remember to date the letter.
2   Write to the Sales Director of De Luxe Drapers Ltd. If you do not know a person's name, write to the specific job title; otherwise the letter is likely to get passed from department to department.
3   Include only those facts you consider relevant. You are prepared to accept delivery, if it is in time, rather than have your money refunded.
4   Sign the letter and print your name underneath. If you are female, it is wise to add Mrs, Miss or Ms in brackets before or after your printed name - eg (Mrs) M Howes. Otherwise people will assume you are a man.

Practice 2 – A thank-you letter

A thank-you letter is often an informal letter. People often ring instead of writing to say thank you, but there are occasions when only a letter will do.

The style can be light, chatty – and witty if you wish. You can use abbreviations like 'don't', 'can't' etc if the letter is to friends or relatives.

Here are the circumstances:

Last Friday you left work to go to another job. You had a bit of a party, with lots of friends and colleagues or workmates, and even the Manager turned up. As well as several personal presents, you had a gift from the whole section, for which they had all contributed.

Write a thank-you letter addressed to the Manager which can be put on the notice board for everyone to read. Follow these instructions:

1   Write from your home address – remember to date the letter.
2   Address it to the Manager by name (make one up).
3   Include the following:

   ● Thanks for the present (decide what it was, and be sure to mention what it was: saying thank you for 'the present' looks as though you have forgotten what it was).
   ● You were very happy to see them all at the party.
   ● You have enjoyed working with them all.
   ● You are looking forward to your new work, but won't forget them.

4   Keep the style light and informal, but because you are writing to the Manager and the letter is going on the notice board, make sure you wouldn't mind who reads it!

Practice 3 – A letter of condolence

When people die, it is often a great comfort to those left behind to receive letters from colleagues, friends and family. These are known as letters of condolence. They are not particularly easy to write, but following a rough format makes it a little less difficult.

You must be sincere in what you say, of course, and the tone needs to be formal without being stilted. The letter need not be a long one and can follow this sort of pattern. The letter should be written as soon as you hear of the death.

(Your address)

(Date)
   Dear _____

   We were/I was so sorry to hear yesterday (today etc) of the death of _____. (You can then say something about it being a shock if the death was sudden, or being a release after a long illness. Avoid saying it was a happy release or a blessed relief!)

(In the second paragraph, say something relevant about the dead person and how much he/she will be missed. Add, if suitable, a sentence about the person to whom you are writing and the family having loved, supported or looked after the dead person. In other words, mention the dead person and those left behind.)

(The third and final paragraph rounds the letter off. You can use either or both the following formal sentences, if appropriate.) Please accept our/my sincere condolences. Our/my thoughts (prayers) are with you at this sad time.

Your sincerely

This is quite a formal letter, as you can see, and if the dead person is a close relative, it is probably too formal. This is the sort of letter you could write to distant relatives, acquaintances or colleagues at work.

Imagine that at work your Supervisor's husband or wife has died suddenly of a heart attack. They have been married about ten years and have two small children. Write a letter of condolence to the Supervisor. Make up the Supervisor's name and the name of the dead person.

Throughout the book you have been asked to write or key the exercises. On this occasion, even if you have keyed in everything else, this is one piece of written work which should be handwritten.

Practice 4 – Poster or leaflet

Adverts in the form of leaflets or posters are quite difficult to write. The tone has to be lively and inviting, without going over the top, and you have to make sure you get all the information in.

The sort of information you must include is:

- the name of the club
- the sort of event (disco, party etc)
- where it is
- when it is (date and starting time)
- cost
- what is included – eg snacks, full buffet etc
- what people should bring (bottle or eats etc)
- what people should come as (fancy dress etc if required)
- any special attractions (live group, spot prizes etc)

In fact you need to make sure people know where they are going, when, why and how much it will cost them.

You also need to encourage them to come. Use drawings and/or slogans to make people want to come – particularly if they are paying!

Design a leaflet or a poster for a Social Club or Sports Club Disco – or any other event. Note that the instruction is 'design' ie you need to think about the layout as well as the words.

Add illustrations or anything you think will make the ad (for that is what it is) attractive.

Practice 5 – Newspaper article

Journalists, whether they write for the tabloids, the heavies or the local newspapers, have a style all their own. They try to write the eye-catching headline, the short, punchy sentence and the interesting nugget of information. They quote what people have said to make their writing seem 'instant' and alive.

Try writing for your own local newspaper. First get hold of a copy of a local paper – the 'freebies' are quite informative.

Choose an event which you would like to see written up in the paper. It could be a match, a celebration, an accident, a fair, a charity collection - anything of local interest.

Write the article following these instructions:
1   Give the whole article a good main heading with one or two sub-headings further down. You might find it easier to write the headings when you have finished the article.
2   Start with an interesting statement or quotation.
    '"I couldn't have had a better day." said 92-year-old Minnie after sky-diving for the first time.' is much more eye-catching than: 'Mrs Minnie Waterton went sky-diving for the first time last Tuesday.'
3   Write the article in short sentences. Give facts and opinions, but make it clear which are which.
4   Keep the paragraphs reasonably short.
5   Add some humour, where applicable.
6   Finish with another interesting quote or statement. 'Minnie is looking forward to scuba diving next.' might make the reader want to read next week's issue.

Practice 6 – Radio script

Scripts, whether they are for plays, commercials or videos, are usually written in the same sort of format. Although the words are written to be spoken, there is no need to use quotation marks. Stage directions are usually written in brackets and often in italics.

Here is an illustration of what a script often looks like. It is the opening of a scene in a radio play: an elderly couple are talking.

(FX) Fade in background music from radio (FX) Whistling kettle	EDWARD:	(*Humming over music*)
(FX) Stop music		What was that you said?
	CELIA:	(*Distant*) I said I hope I shall be able to get some brown bread tomorrow, there's always such a queue at the bakers on Christmas Eve.
	EDWARD:	Oh, I dare say you will – you usually do.
(FX) Crockery	CELIA:	Yes. Hadn't you better be getting your coat on, Edward? You'll be late.
	EDWARD:	Oh, there's no hurry.
	CELIA:	(*Close*) Well, it's a quarter to, and it takes you a good ten minutes to walk up the hill. You won't have any breath left to sing.
	EDWARD:	Well, ... I'm not going tonight.

You will see that the sound effects (FX) are written on the left. The stage directions are written within brackets and italics to make it obvious they are not dialogue.

Write a short script for a radio commercial, following these instructions:

1   The company you want to promote is Sunspots, which specialises in package holidays round the Mediterranean. It has a special offer of cheap holidays in Spain.

2   Use three characters:

- one male
- one female
- one voiceover (can be M or F) to give the details of the holidays. He or she might finish with something like:
  VOICEOVER: Book with Sunspots through your travel agent N-O-W or ring 0800 021 021 for details.

3   It will probably be easiest to work in this sequence:

- Write an outline of the scene: where it is set, who the characters are, the storyline of what they are going to say and what the voiceover will say.
- Write the script of the actual dialogue – the words each one is to say. This is where you can really write as people speak, not in formal English.
- Add any stage directions eg (*Whispering*) (*Shouting*) etc.
- Add in the FX – seagulls?!

4   Get it keyed in. It is almost impossible to read scripts from handwriting.

When you have completed it, have a recording session and see what it sounds like. Ask three of your friends to do the voices and others to do the FX.

Points to remember from this chapter

- Consider the reader: put yourself in the reader's shoes and see whether what you have written is right for that reader.
- Check spelling, grammar and punctuation. If it is wrong it lessens the impact of what you have written.
- Use the right format for the right occasion.
- Use the right tone and style. Do not be chatty when you should be formal. You need never be long-winded or boring.
- Live up to your image. Presentation is important.

Appendix 1: Commonly misspelled words

absence
absorption
access
accessible
accommodation
achievement
acknowledge
acquaintance
acquiesce
acquisition
address
aggravate
agreeable
amateur
analysis
   (pl. analyses)
ancillary
anonymous
anxiety
apparent
appearance
appropriate
argument
arrangement
assess
assiduous
assist
awful

bachelor
beginning
believed
benefited
breathe

budgeted
bureau
bureaucracy
business

category
chaos
colleague
commitment
committed
committee
comparative
compatible
competence
connoisseur
conscientious
conscious
consistent
convenience
correlate
correspondence
correspondent
corroborate
courteous
courtesy

deceive
deficient
definite
dependant (noun)
dependent
   (adjective)
desirable
deterrent

disappear
disappoint
discipline
discreet
discrepancy
dissatisfied
distributor

efficiency
eighth
eliminated
embarrassment
eminent
enthusiasm
equipment
equipped
erroneous
especially
essential
exaggerated
excellent
exercise
exhausted
experience
extremely

favourite
feasible
financial
foreign
forty
fulfil
fulfilled
fulfilment

gauge
government
grievance
guarantee
guard

harassment
height
heroes
honorary
honour
humorous
humour
hypocrisy
hypothesis
   (pl. hypotheses)

immediately
immigrant
imminent
incidentally
incipient
independent
indispensable
influential
install
instalment
intelligence
irrelevant
irreparable
irresistible
judg(e)ment
judicial

knowledge	permanent	quiet	suppress
	permissible		surprising
liaison	persevere	received	synonymous
losing	personnel	recommend	synonyms
lying	persuade	reference	
	piece	referred	technical
maintenance	planning	relieved	technology
manoeuvre	possess	repetition	temporary
marriage	potential	responsibility	tendency
Mediterranean	precede		transfer
	preceding	scarcely	transference
necessary	predecessor	seize	transferred
negotiable	preference	sentence	transient
niece	preferred	separate	twelfth
noticeable	preliminary	siege	
	prestige	similar	unconscious
occasionally	privilege	sincerely	underrated
occur	procedure	skilful	undoubtedly
occurred	professional	statutory	unfortunately
occurrence	professor	subtle	
omission	pronunciation	subtlety	warehouse
omit	proprietary	succeed	weird
omitted	psychology	successful	wield
	pursue	successfully	withhold
parallel		summary	woollen
parliament	questionnaire	supersede	
			yield

Appendix 2: Confusibles

accept/except 'To accept' is a verb, eg 'Yes, I'll accept your offer.' 'Except' is a preposition, eg 'Everyone's going except me.'

adverse/averse Both these words are adjectives showing a degree of hostility, eg 'The launch met an adverse reception; they were averse to the product.' 'Adverse' is stronger than 'averse'. 'Averse' is usually used in the form 'he is averse to...'

advice/advise 'Advice' is the noun, eg 'Please accept my advice.' 'Advise' is the verb, eg 'Please advise me on this problem.'

affect/effect 'Affect' is almost always used as a verb, eg 'That wine affected me badly.' 'Effect' can be used as a noun, eg 'That wine had a bad effect on me.' It can also be used as a verb when it means to bring something about, eg 'To effect a reconciliation' means to make a reconciliation happen.

alternately/alternatively 'Alternately' means 'one after the other', eg 'When you walk you use alternate feet.' 'Alternatively' means 'in the alternative' where someone has a choice between two possibilities, eg 'You can have soup or, alternatively, you can have a prawn cocktail.'

ante/anti These are both prefixes. 'Ante' means before, as in ante-natal'. 'Anti' means against, as in 'anti-smoking'.

borrow/lend *See 'lend' below.*

censer/censor/censure 'A censer' is an object for holding incense, usually used in churches. 'To censor' is to edit as in the British Board of Film Censors. 'To censure' is to criticise unfavourably or to judge something.

complement/compliment 'To complement' something is to make it complete. 'To compliment' someone is to praise them. Free tickets are complimentary ones.

council/counsel 'A Council' is a noun, as in Local Council of which a member is a Councillor. 'Counsel' may be a verb or a noun. 'To counsel someone' is to give them advice, as does a Relate Counsellor. When used as a noun it means advice or, when referring to a person, a barrister.

disinterested/uninterested Someone who is disinterested is acting impartially, not out of self-interest. Someone who is uninterested is bored.

effect/affect *See 'affect' above.*

emigrant/immigrant Which of these words you use to describe someone moving from one country to another depends on your point of view. If that person is leaving the country you are in, she or he will be an emigrant. If she or he is entering the country you are in, he or she is an immigrant.

eminent/imminent An eminent person is an important or famous one. An imminent event is one which is about to happen.

enquire/inquire There is little difference between these two words. 'To enquire' is to ask whereas 'to inquire' is to ask more searchingly. You may enquire about the time of the next train; the police conduct inquiries into crimes.

ensure/insure 'To ensure' is to make sure. To insure something is to take out an insurance policy on it, eg, 'I have ensured that all my possessions are insured.'

especially/specially *See 'specially' below.*

except/accept *See 'accept' above.*

formally/formerly 'Formally is the opposite of 'informally', whereas 'formerly' means previously.

immigrant/emigrant *See 'emigrant' above.*

imminent/eminent *See 'eminent' above.*

imply/infer 'To imply' something is to convey it without saying it explicitly. 'To infer' something is to deduce it from the given facts.

inquire/enquire *See 'enquire' above.*

insure/ensure *See 'ensure' above.*

it's/its 'It's' means 'it is'. The apostrophe shows the letter 'i' is missing. 'Its' is the equivalent of 'my', 'her', 'their' etc, when applied to a thing, eg 'The door's come off its hinge. It's useless now.'

lend/borrow The owner 'lends'; the borrower 'borrows'. Lend 'to', borrow 'from'.

lie/lay To 'lie' is to tell a lie or lie down; you do this yourself. To 'lay' is to put someone or something down; you do it to something or someone else.

peace/piece 'Peace' is the absence of war or noise, 'piece' is a bit or part (bits and pieces).

personal/personnel 'Personnel' is concerned with a lot of people (a Company's personnel); 'personal' is private.

practice/practise 'Practice' is the noun, eg, 'Some practice would help you improve.' 'Practise' is the verb, eg 'You must practise if you want to improve.' The same rule applies as for 'advice' and 'advise'.

precede/proceed 'To precede' is to go before, eg 'The meeting will be preceded by lunch.' 'To proceed' is to go ahead, eg 'Please proceed with the meeting without me.'

principal/principle Where 'principal' is used as a noun it means the head of something, eg, of a training college. Where 'principal' is used as an adjective it means 'main', or 'chief', eg 'The principal reason for the drop in sales is the difficulty in delivering on time.' 'Principle' is always used as a noun. It means a fundamental belief, eg, 'I never work on Sundays on principle.'

sight/site 'Sight' is to do with eyes and seeing; 'site' is to do with a place or location (this is IT).

specially/especially 'Specially' means for a particular purpose, eg 'This was made specially for you.' 'Especially' means unusually or to a high degree, eg

'This is especially good work.'

stationary/stationery 'Stationary' means unmoving, fixed – it is an adjective. 'Stationery' is a noun referring to pens, paper etc. 'Stationary' stands still; 'stationery' includes envelopes.

storey/story 'Storey' means floor as in 'a five-storey building'. 'Story' means tale as in 'fairy story'.

teach/learn Teachers 'teach' things to others. Learners 'learn' things from others. (Teachers teach and Learners learn.)

their/there/they're Their is the equivalent of 'his' or 'her' when referring to more than one person. 'There' is the opposite of 'here'. 'They're is 'they are' with an apostrophe to show the 'a' is missing.

to/too/two 'To' is used as in 'going to a place'. 'Too' is used to show an excess or for emphasis, eg 'Too many cooks spoil the broth.' 'Two' equals 2.

where/were 'Where' is to do with place eg 'Where?' – 'There!' 'Were' is part of the verb 'to be' – 'we were'.

whether/weather 'Whether' means 'if'. 'Weather' is about the climate, eg 'I wonder whether the weather will be fine.'

whose/who's 'Whose' is used to show possession of something, eg 'The person whose office is on the ground floor . . . Whose office is it?' 'Who's' is the equivalent of 'who is'.

Index

GREENWICH EXCHANGE BOOKS

STUDENT GUIDES

Greenwich Exchange Student Guides are critical studies of major or contemporary serious writers in English and selected European languages. The series is for the Student, the Teacher and the 'common reader' and are ideal resources for libraries. The *Times Educational Supplement (TES)* praised these books saying, "The style of these guides has a pressure of meaning behind it. Students should learn from that... If art is about selection, perception and taste, then this is it."

(ISBN prefix 1-871551- applies)
The series includes:
W. H. Auden by Stephen Wade (-36-6)
William Blake by Peter Davies (-27-7)
The Brontës by Peter Davies (-24-2)
Joseph Conrad by Martin Seymour-Smith (-18-8)
William Cowper by Michael Thorn (-25-0)
Charles Dickens by Robert Giddings (-26-9)
John Donne by Sean Haldane (-23-4)
Thomas Hardy by Sean Haldane (-35-1)
Seamus Heaney by Warren Hope (-37-4)
Philip Larkin by Warren Hope (-35-8)
Shakespeare's Non-Dramatic Poetry (22-6)
Tobias Smollett by Robert Giddings (-21-8)
Alfred Lord Tennyson by Michael Thorn (-20-X)
Wordsworth by Andrew Keanie (57-9)

OTHER GREENWICH EXCHANGE BOOKS

All paperbacks unless otherwise stated.

POETRY

Adam's Thoughts in Winter *by Warren Hope*
Warren Hope's poems have appeared from time to time in a number of literary periodicals, pamphlets, and anthologies on both sides of the Atlantic. They appeal to lovers of poetry everywhere. His poems are brief, clear, frequently lyrical, characterised by wit, but often distinguished by tenderness. The poems gathered in this first book-length collection counter the brutalising ethos of contemporary life, speaking of and for the virtues of modesty, honesty, and gentleness in an individual, memorable way. Hope was born in Philadelphia where he raised his family and continues to live near there. He is the author of critical studies of Shakespeare and Larkin and is the biographer of Norman Cameron, the British poet and translator.
ISBN 1-871551-40-4; A5 size; 54pp

Baudelaire: Les Fleurs du Mal in English Verse
translated by F. W. Leakey
Selected poems from *Les Fleurs du Mal* are translated with parallel French texts, are designed to be read with pleasure by readers who have no French, as well as those practised in the French language.
F. W. Leakey is Emeritus Professor of French in the University of London. As a scholar, critic and teacher he has specialised in the work of Baudelaire for 50 years. He has published a number of books on Baudelaire.
ISBN 1-871551-10-2; A5 size; 140pp

Lines from the Stone Age *by Sean Haldane*
Reviewing Sean Haldane's 1992 volume *Desire in Belfast* Robert Nye wrote in *The Times* that 'Haldane can be sure of his place among the English poets.' The facts that his early volumes appeared in Canada and that he has earned his living by other means than literature have meant that this place is not yet a conspicuous one, although his poems have always had their circle of readers. The 60 previously unpublished poems of *Lines from the Stone Age* – 'lines of longing, terror, pride, lust and pain' – may widen this circle.
ISBN 1-871551-39-0; A5 size; 58pp

Wilderness *by Martin Seymour-Smith*
This is Seymour-Smith's first publication of his poetry for more than 20 years. This collection of 36 poems is a fearless account of an inner life of love, frustration, guilt, laughter and the celebration of others. Best known to the general public as the author of the controversial and best selling *Hardy* (1994).
ISBN 1-871551-08-0; A5 size; 64pp

LITERATURE & BIOGRAPHY
The Author, the Book & the Reader *by Robert Giddings*
This collection of essays analyses the effects of changing technology and the attendant commercial pressures on literary styles and subject matter. Authors covered include Dickens; Smollett; Mark Twain; Dr Johnson; John Le Carré.
ISBN 1-871551-01-0; A5 size; 220pp; illus.

The Good That We Do *by John Lucas*
John Lucas's new book blends fiction, biography and social history in order to tell the story of the grandfather he never knew. Horace Kelly was born in Torquay in 1880 and died sixty years later, soon after the outbreak of the second world war. Headteacher of a succession of elementary schools in impoverished areas of London during the first part of the 20th century, "Hod" Kelly was also a keen cricketer, a devotee of the music hall, and included among his friends the great Trade Union leader, Ernest Bevin. In telling the story of his life, Lucas has provided a fascinating

range of insights into the lives of ordinary Londoners: their entertainments, domestic arrangements, experiences of the privations of war, including the aerial bombardments of 1917 and 1918, and their growing realisation during the 1920s and 1930s that they were doomed to suffer it all again. Threaded through is an account of such people's hunger for education, and of the different ways government, church and educational officialdom ministered to that hunger. *The Good That We Do* is both a study of one man and of a period when England was changed, drastically and for ever.
ISBN 1-871551-54-4; A5 size, 218pp

In Pursuit of Lewis Carroll *by Raphael Shaberman*

Sherlock Holmes and the author uncover new evidence in their investigations into the mysterious life and writing of Lewis Carroll. They examine published works by Carroll that have been overlooked by previous commentators. A newly discovered poem, almost certainly by Carroll, is published here. Amongst many aspects of Carroll's highly complex personality, this book explores his relationship with his parents, numerous child friends, and the formidable Mrs Liddell, mother of the immortal Alice.
ISBN 1-871551-13-7; 70% A4 size; 130pp; illus.

Laughter in the Dark – The Plays of Joe Orton *by Arthur Burke*

Arthur Burke examines the two facets of Joe Orton. Orton the playwright had a rare ability to delight and shock audiences with such outrageous farces as *Loot* and *What the Butler Saw*. Orton the man was a promiscuous homosexual caught up in a destructive relationship with a jealous and violent older man. In this study – often as irreverent as the plays themselves – Burke dissects Orton's comedy and traces the connection between the lifestyle and the work. Previously a television critic and comedian, Arthur Burke is a writer and journalist. He has published articles not only on Orton but also on Harold Pinter, John Osborne and many other leading modern dramatists.
ISBN 1-981551-56-0; A5 size 100pp

Liar! Liar!: Jack Kerouac – Novelist *by R. J. Ellis*

The fullest study of Jack Kerouac's fiction to date. It is the first book to devote an individual chapter to each and every one of his novels. *On the Road, Visions of Cody* and *The Subterraneans*, Kerouac's central masterpieces, are re-read indepth, in a new and exciting way. The books Kerouac himself saw as major elements of his spontaneous 'bop' odyssey, *Visions of Gerard* and *Doctor Sax*, are also strikingly reinterpreted, as are other, daringly innovative writings, like *The Railroad Earth* and his 'try at a spontaneous *Finnegans Wake*', *Old Angel Midnight*. Undeservedly neglected writings, such as *Tristessa* and *Big Sur*, are also analysed, alongside better known novels like *Dharma Bums* and *Desolation Angels*.

Liar! Liar! takes its title for the words of *Tristessa's* narrator, Jack, referring to himself. He also warns us 'I guess, I'm a liar, watch out!'. R. J. Ellis' study provocatively proposes that we need to take this warning seriously and, rather than reading Kerouac's novels simply as fictional versions of his life, focus just as much on the way the novels stand as variations on a series of ambiguously-represented themes: explorations of class, sexual identity, the French-Canadian Catholic confessional, and addiction in its hydra-headed modern forms. Ellis shows how Kerouac's deep anxieties in each of these arenas makes him an incisive commentator on his uncertain times and a bitingly honest self-critic, constantly attacking his narrators' 'vanities'.

R. J. Ellis is Professor of English and American Studies at the Nottingham Trent University. His commentaries on Beat writing have been frequently published, and his most recent book, a full modern edition of Harriet Wilson's *Our Nig*, the first ever novel by an African American woman, has been widely acclaimed.
ISBN 1-871551-53-6; A5 size; 300pp

Norman Cameron *by Warren Hope*
Cameron's poetry was admired by Auden; celebrated by Dylan Thomas; valued by Robert Graves. He was described by Martin Seymour-Smith as "one of... the most rewarding and pure poets of his generation..." and is at last given a full length biography. This eminently sociable man, who had periods of darkness and despair, wrote little poetry by comparison with others of his time, but always of a high and consistent quality – imaginative and profound.
ISBN 1-871551-05-6; A5 size; 250pp; illus.

Musical Offering *by Yolanthe Leigh*
In a series of vivid sketches, anecdotes and reflections, Yolanthe Leigh tells the story of her growing up in the Poland of the nineteen thirties and the second world war. These are poignant episodes of a child's first encounters with both the enchantments and the cruelties of the world; and from a later time, stark memories of the brutality of the Nazi invasion, and the hardships of student life in Warsaw under the Occupation. But most of all this is a record of inward development; passages of remarkable intensity and simplicity describe the girl's response to religion, to music, and to her discovery of philosophy.

The outcome is something unique, a book that eludes classification. In its own distinctive fashion, it creates a memorable picture of a highly perceptive and sensitive individual, set against a background of national tragedy.
ISBN 1-871551-46-3; A5 size 61pp

Shakespeare's Non-Dramatic Poetry *by Martin Seymour-Smith*
In this study, completed shortly before his death in 1998, Martin Seymour-Smith sheds fresh light on two very different groups of Shakespeare's non-dramatic poems:

the early and conventional *Venus and Adonis* and *The Rape of Lucrece*, and the highly personal *Sonnets*. He explains the genesis of the first two in the genre of Ovidian narrative poetry in which a young Elizabethan man of letters was expected to excel, and which was highly popular. In the *Sonnets* (his 1963 old-spelling edition of which is being reissued by Greenwich Exchange) he traces the mental journey of a man going through an acute psychological crisis as he faces up to the truth about his own unconventional sexuality.

It is a study which confronts those 'disagreeables' in the *Sonnets* which most critics have ignored.

ISBN 1-871551-22-6; A5 size; 90pp

Shakespeare's Sonnets *edited by Martin Seymour-Smith*

Martin Seymour-Smith's outstanding achievement lies in the field of literary biography and criticism. In 1963 he produced his comprehensive edition, in the old spelling of *Shakespeare's Sonnets* (here revised and corrected by him and Peter Davies in 1998). With its landmark introduction, it was praised by William Empson and John Dover Wilson. Stephen Spender said of him: "I greatly admire Martin Seymour-Smith for the independence of his views and the great interest of his mind;" and both Robert Graves and Anthony Burgess described him as the leading critic of his time. His exegesis of the Sonnets remains unsurpassed.

ISBN 1-871551-38-2; A5 size; 200pp

PHILOSOPHY

Deals and Ideals *by James Daly*

Alasdair MacIntyre writes of this book: "In his excellent earlier book *Marx: Justice and Dialectic* James Daly identified Marx's place in and extraordinary contribution to the moral debates of the modern era. Now he has put us even further in his debt not only by relating Marx to his Aristotelian predecessors and to the natural law tradition, but also by using this understanding of Marx to throw fresh light on the moral antagonism between Marx and individualist conceptions of human nature. This is a splendid sequel to his earlier work".

ISBN 1-87155-31-5; A5 size; 160pp

Marx: Justice and Dialectic *by James Daly*

Department of Scholastic Philosophy, Queen's University, Belfast. James Daly shows the humane basis of Marx's thinking, rather than the imposed 'economic materialistic' views of many modern commentators. In particular he refutes the notion that for Marx, justice relates simply to the state of development of society at a particular time. Marx's views about justice and human relationships belong to the continuing traditions of moral thought in Europe.

ISBN 1-871551-28-5; A5 size; 180pp

The Philosophy of Whitehead *by T. E. Burke*
Department of Philosophy, University of Reading.
Dr Burke explores the main achievements of this philosopher, better known in the US than Britain. Whitehead, often remembered as Russell's tutor and collaborator on *Principia Mathematica,* was one of the few who had a grasp of relativity and its possible implications. His philosophical writings reflect his profound knowledge of mathematics and science. He was responsible for initiating process theology.
ISBN 1-871551-29-3; A5 size; 106pp

Questions of Platonism *by Ian Leask*
In a daring challenge to contemporary orthodoxy, Ian Leask subverts both Hegel and Heidegger by arguing for a radical re-evaluation of Platonism. Thus, while he traces a profoundly Platonic continuity between ancient Athens and 19th century Germany, the nature of this Platonism, he suggests, is neither 'totalizing' nor Hegelian but, instead, open-ended 'incomplete' and oriented towards a divine goal beyond *logos* or any metaphysical structure. Such a re-evaluation exposes the deep anti-Platonism of Hegel's absolutizing of volitional subjectivity; it also confirms Schelling as true modern heir to the 'constitutive incompletion' of Plato and Plotinus. By providing a more nuanced approach - refusing to accept either Hegel's self-serving account of 'Platonism' or the (equally totalizing) post-Heideggerian inversion of this narrative – Leask demonstrates the continued relevance of a genuine, 'finite' Platonic quest. Ian Leask teaches in the Department of Scholastic Philosophy at the Queen's University of Belfast.
ISBN 1-871551-32-3; A5 size; 154pp

FICTION
The Case of the Scarlet Woman – Sherlock Holmes and the Occult
by Watkin Jones
A haunted house, a mysterious kidnapping and a poet's demonic visions are just the beginnings of three connected cases that lead Sherlock Holmes into confrontation with the infamous black magician Aleister Crowley and, more sinisterly, his scorned Scarlet Woman.
The fact that Dr Watson did not publish details of these investigations is perhaps testament to the unspoken fear he and Holmes harboured for the supernatural. *The Case of the Scarlet Woman* convinced them both that some things cannot be explained by cold logic.
ISBN 1-871551-14-5; A5 size; 130pp

THEATRE
Music Hall Warriors: A history of the Variety Artistes Federation
by Peter Honri
This is an unique and fascinating history of how vaudeville artistes formed the first effective actor's trade union in 1906 and then battled with the powerful owners of

music halls to obtain fairer contracts. The story continues with the VAF dealing with performing rights, radio, and the advent of television. Peter Honri is the fourth generation of a vaudeville family. The book has a foreword by the Right Honourable John Major MP when he was Prime Minister – his father was a founder member of the VAF.

ISBN 1-871551-06-4; A4 size; 140pp; illus.